P9-CMQ-514

HAWAII: The Aloha State

BY BEN ADAMS

ALASKA: THE BIG LAND

HAWAII

The Aloha State

Our Island Democracy in Text and Pictures

by BEN ADAMS

HILL AND WANG • NEW YORK

FIRST PRINTING NOVEMBER 1959

SECOND PRINTING JANUARY 1960

LIBRARY OF CONGRESS CATALOG CARD NUMBER: 59-15072

MANUFACTURED IN THE UNITED STATES OF AMERICA

Acknowledgments

For the photographs reproduced here by permission, the author extends thanks to the Archives of Hawaii for pictures on pages 7, 18, 23, 24, 25, 27, 28, 33, 41, 42, 47, 48, 49, 52, 53, 54, 56, 57, 58, 59, 68, and 136; Bernice P. Bishop Museum, Baker Collection for those on pages 30, 32, 37, and 39; Dole Pineapple Co., pages 10, 62, 64, and 66; Hawaiian Pineapple Co., pages 63 and 65; Hawaiian Sugar Planters Association, pages 13, 60, 94, 95, 96, 109, and 114; Hawaii Visitors Bureau, pages iii, 2 (bottom), 4, 5, 6, 8, 9, 11, 12, 15, 17, 19, 21, 45, 51, 61, 67, 89, 92, 97, 98, 99, 100, 108, 113, 115, 116, 117, 118, 119, 122, 123, 126, 131, 135, 138, 140, 141, 142, 143, 147, 151, 152, 159, 160, 163, 165, 166, 167, 168, 169, 170, 171, 172, 173, 174, 177, 178, 181, 182, 183, 184, 185, 191, 193, 194, 195, 196, 197, 198, 199, and 200; Honolulu Academy of Arts, pages 153, 158, 186, 187, and 188; ILWU, pages 80, 85, 86, 87, 130, 150, and 180; Official U.S. Navy Photograph, pages 71, 75, 76, 77, 78, 101, 102, and 104; Photo Hawaii, page 189; Teamsters Union, pages 83 and 157; The Pineapple Companies of Hawaii, page 112; University of Hawaii, pages 2 (top), 14, 139, 144, 145, and 155; and Wide World Photos, page 132.

The photographs on the jacket of the cloth-bound edition are used with the following permissions: front and left column of back jacket, Hawaii Visitors Bureau; and back jacket, right column, Hawaiian Pineapple Company; all photographs on cover of paperback edition, Hawaii Visitors Bureau.

Contents

HAWAII:
The Aloha State

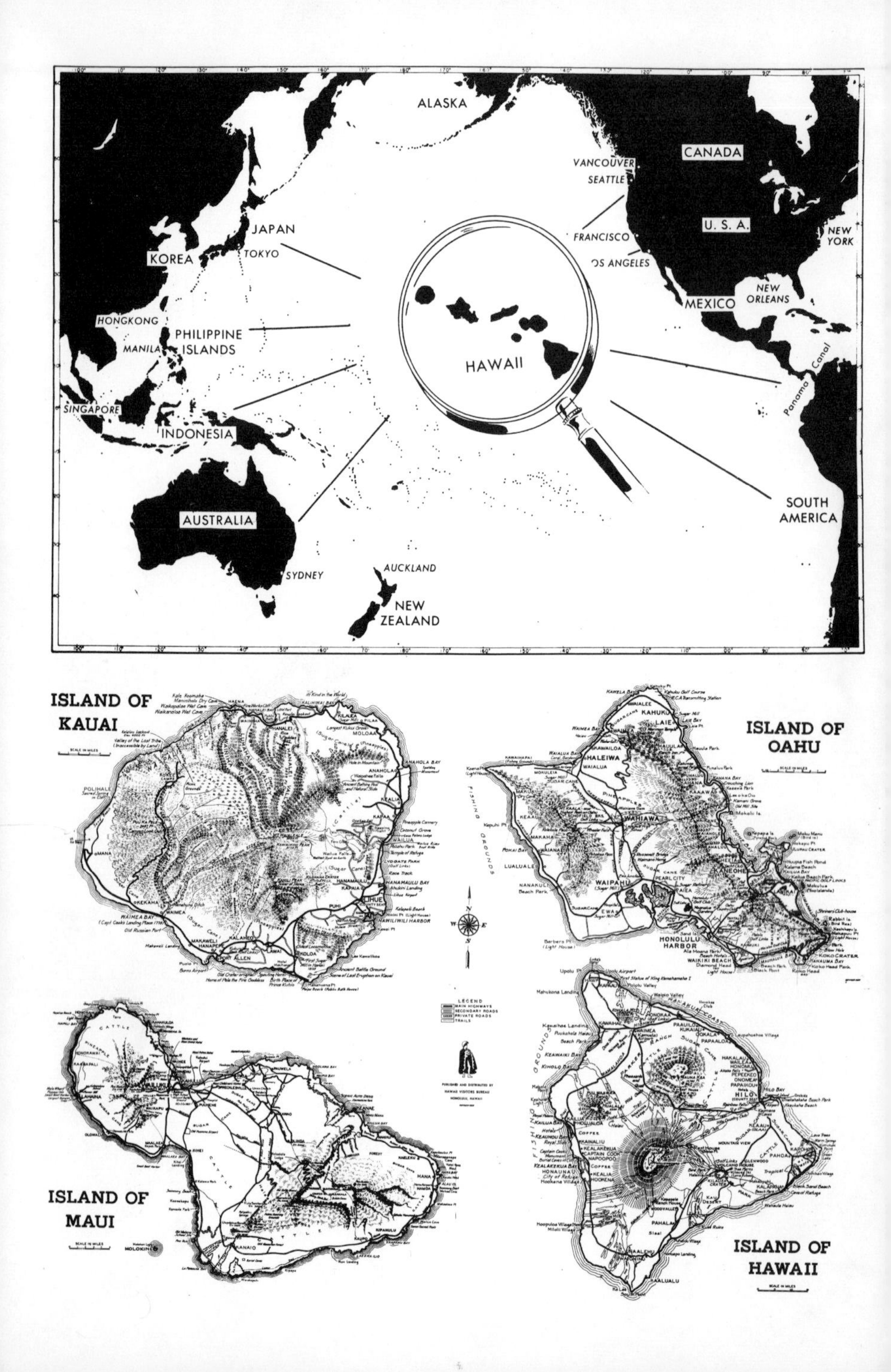
ALASKA
CANADA
VANCOUVER
SEATTLE
FRANCISCO
U. S. A.
NEW YORK
OS ANGELES
NEW ORLEANS
MEXICO
JAPAN
TOKYO
KOREA
HONGKONG
PHILIPPINE ISLANDS
MANILA
HAWAII
SINGAPORE
INDONESIA
Panama Canal
SOUTH AMERICA
AUSTRALIA
SYDNEY
AUCKLAND
NEW ZEALAND
ISLAND OF KAUAI
ISLAND OF OAHU
ISLAND OF MAUI
ISLAND OF HAWAII
LEGEND
MAIN HIGHWAYS
SECONDARY ROADS
PRIVATE ROADS
TRAILS
PUBLISHED AND DISTRIBUTED BY
HAWAII VISITORS BUREAU
HONOLULU, HAWAII

1. *"Loveliest Fleet of Islands"*

A distinguished anthropologist from the mainland, visiting one of Honolulu's schools, was fascinated by its rich mixture of students from diverse racial and national backgrounds. He was particularly struck by the close attention being given by a class made up largely of Oriental children to a pictorial display about the landing of the Pilgrims on the rock-bound coast of Massachusetts.

"What are you looking at, little girl?" he asked an intent Chinese third-grader.

"I am studying about the history of our Pilgrim Fathers," the girl replied in precise and solemn tones.

The anthropologist pauses thoughtfully when he tells the story. "Yes, they are her Pilgrim Fathers," he says, "just as her Confucian ancestors are her fathers too."

If this story is part of the folklore of Hawaii, it is also part of its reality. Any visitor, taking a bus from the white sand beaches and the luxury hotels of Waikiki to downtown Honolulu, will be as struck as the learned anthropologist was by the exciting blend of people and cultures.

You will see a bewildering variety of peoples of subtly different colors and shapes: short, slender Japanese; tall, husky Hawaiians; dark-skinned Filipinos; and the intriguing mixtures

Hawaii's children

of Chinese-Hawaiian or Portuguese-Japanese as well as many others more intricate and involved. You will see some of the world's most beautiful women, slightly mysterious to the mainlander because so many of them defy the conventional racial tags, their colors and features representing a blending of Hawaii's peoples; their clothing ranging from the shapeless but colorful muumuus to tight-fitting Chinese sheaths and stylish American clothes.

Downtown you will see the squat old buildings occupied by the historic companies which run Hawaii's sugar plantations — and new glass-fronted skyscrapers rising everywhere. Nearby you will see little Japanese restaurants and delicatessens. You will see modern department stores and supermarkets — and a few blocks away you can wander into venerable, sprawling food stores featuring every conceivable variety of Oriental and Ha-

Honolulu's harbor and downtown area

waiian fish and meat and vegetables, seaweed and beancake and poi.

The real Hawaii is perhaps different in some respects from the Hawaii you expect from picture postcards and travel brochures. But it is no less wonderful or beautiful; and perhaps more exciting and varied and complex.

Hawaii is a modern industrial and agricultural community — peopled by an exotic mixture of races and cultures — and all set down in a South Sea island setting. Literal-minded tourists may be disappointed in their failure to find primitive natives in their natural habitat. The grass-skirted hula girl routine has been overdone. Even the most naïve will soon discover that he is watching the synthetic motions of sophisticated city girls rather than ancient aboriginal rites. The heavy traffic in Honolulu, the modern office buildings, and the construction boom may come as something of a surprise. But the setting comes up to advance

Hula dancers in front of grass shack in Honolulu park

billing. Mark Twain once described Hawaii as "the loveliest fleet of Islands that lies anchored in any ocean." The description still defies improvement.

The islands almost literally rose out of the sea, and that is how they strike you as you see them for the first time from the air or from aboard ship. Endless millions of years ago, but relatively recently as geological time is reckoned, the floor of the Pacific cracked open for almost two thousand miles. Out of the rift spewed sea and steam and fiery basalt rock. As rock piled upon rock, mountains were formed – some starting 18,000 feet below sea level and building up in some cases as high as 14,000 feet above the sea. The Hawaii islands were formed on the tops of the emerging volcanic mountains, and around the edges of the islands countless tiny coral animals built up reefs extending into

Jack London and his wife in Hawaii

the ocean. During the ice age the islands were covered with great frozen sheets, and when the icecaps melted the mountains were again submerged by water.

Out of the endless volcanic flow and the interaction of fire and sea and wind and ice came the fabled islands which won the hearts of Mark Twain and Robert Louis Stevenson and Jack London and of millions of less gifted wanderers on the earth. There came white coral beaches, surrounded by palm trees and overhung by sheer cliffs. There came perfect little semicircular beaches in the mouths of extinct volcanoes, and black beaches pounded by the waves from volcanic rock. There came fertile valleys planted now in sugar cane and pineapple, and deep gorges such as Iao Valley on Maui with its green-covered rock needle rising 1,200 feet into the air. There came the desert and the grazing land and the volcanic pits on the Big Island of Hawaii, and the tropical forests only a few miles away. There came the great fern trees, the silverswords with long, narrow, shimmering leaves and hundreds of tiny purple blossoms. There

This giant monkeypot tree covers close to an acre

grew luxuriantly the bright-hued hibiscus and the orchid and Hawaii's innumerable other flowers and plants.

For more than 1,500 miles into the Pacific, far to the Northwest, to Midway and Kure Islands where warships fought a decisive battle in World War II, extends this island fleet. There are 23 islands in all, but some are mere coral reefs or sand shoals or jagged rocks. The term Hawaiian Islands usually refers to only eight of the islands of which the two outermost are only about 300 miles apart. The total area of the islands which form our fiftieth state is 6,435 square miles, small enough to be tucked away in a corner of Texas or Alaska but bigger than Rhode Island, Delaware, or Connecticut.

Oahu is the island most people visit when they go to Hawaii.

A chain of craters on Maui's Haleakala volcano

Here are Honolulu and Waikiki Beach. Here is the metropolis of the new state, its commercial, political, and tourist center. Hawaii, generally called the Big Island, has almost two thirds of the new state's territory. It boasts active volcanoes, huge mountains, giant cattle ranches, and tiny coffee farms.

Maui is called the "valley isle" because of its fertile valley in between the volcanic mountain masses on the east and west.

Kauai, the "garden isle," is known for its flowers and for Waimea Canyon, which has been described as the Grand Canyon of the Pacific.

Fields of sugar cane are seen almost everywhere on these four islands, the biggest and most populated of the Hawaiian chain. On two smaller islands pineapple is predominant. One of these is Molokai, which is shaped something like an Indian moccasin. Here is also found the settlement for victims of Hansen's disease – leprosy – made famous by Father Damien. The other is Lanai

A terraced pineapple field

on top of an extinct volcano. Lanai used to be grassy pasture land, but has been transformed since the early 1920's into a great fertile plantation owned entirely by the Hawaiian Pineapple Company.

The remaining two islands are important chiefly as curiosities. Kahoolawe is barren and uninhabited. Once the site of a penal colony in the days of the Hawaiian monarchy, it is now used for target practice by United States warships and planes. Niihau, privately owned, is sometimes called the "mystery island." It has been shut off from the outside world and maintained as a sanctuary of the old Hawaii, inhabited by the last surviving community of pure Hawaiians who speak their ancient language and adhere to a now vanishing way of life.

One of the wonders of Hawaii, and one of its major natural resources, is, of course, its climate. It is gently languorous rather than oppressive, warm rather than hot, subtropical rather than

There is even skiing – not too often – on the slopes of Mauna Kea, the great extinct volcano on Hawaii, the Big Island

tropical. Trade winds and ocean currents cool the islands, which are in the same latitude as Central America, Burma, and French West Africa. There are substantial variations in temperature and climate for so small an area. There is rainfall of as much as 400 inches a year in some places – and very little only a few miles away. There is snow on the mountain peaks of the Big Island – and arid desert below. The average year-round temperature in the lowlands, including Honolulu, is about 75 degrees Fahrenheit; less in the mountains.

It is no less a wonder that on these tropical islands, so often called the Paradise of the Pacific, there should have developed an up-to-date twentieth-century civilization and a billion-dollar economy – about $1.5 billion in business transactions in 1959.

The early missionaries and traders and sailors soon discovered how fertile was Hawaii's soil and how well suited for sugar cane.

A recently planted pineapple field

Later came the importation of the exotic pineapple from the West Indies. Hawaii became a country of great plantations, worked by imported Asian labor. The plantations are still there, and still fertile. But now they are surpassed in dollar volume by military expenditures, rivaled by tourism and construction as major industries. New crops and new manufactures have begun to develop. Besides, the plantations themselves have changed. They have become modernized and mechanized, their work performed not by multitudes of unskilled cheap labor but by a relatively few thousand skilled, highly paid, and solidly unionized workers.

The change on the plantations is part of the larger change that has come about in Hawaii, mainly since World War II. In only a few short years Hawaii has catapulted from a semifeudal economic languor into the bustle of a modern industrial society, from control by a handful of well-established families into a more rounded and competitive economy, into a democratic community with active participation by varied peoples and races in all aspects of life, into a community with a high rate of literacy, advanced social legislation, and an active citizenry.

The very suddenness of the transformation has resulted in startling contrasts. While Honolulu has become a great modern

Sugar mill and surrounding plantation community

city, relatively primitive fishing villages are still to be found on some of the outer islands. Old handicrafts are still practiced — and often not too far from industries using the latest and most advanced techniques. There is still poverty among some of Hawaii's people as well as glittering wealth. Honolulu has run-down slums as well as handsome and prosperous suburbs. At least some knowledge of how Hawaii changed and developed is necessary for these contrasts to be understood. But certainly the most startling and significant thing is the change itself, the fact that Hawaii is predominantly a modern community and rapidly becoming more so.

Hawaii has many assets: its soil, its scenic beauty, its mid-Pacific setting. Perhaps its greatest resource is its people. In listing the four factors that "have been basic in making Hawaii what it is today," a Bank of Hawaii bulletin, hardly an organ of "do-gooder" sentimentality, puts people first, stating: "People of diverse racial origins brought to the islands a wide range of cultural backgrounds, inherent abilities, and contacts with other parts of the world."

Who are Hawaii's 600,000 people, and where do they come from? One estimate, accepted as reasonably accurate by Dr.

Students of many races at the University of Hawaii

Andrew W. Lind of the University of Hawaii, is that 34 percent are Japanese in origin, 25 percent Caucasian, 20 percent Hawaiian and part-Hawaiian, 12 percent Filipino, 6 percent Chinese, 2 percent Puerto Rican, 1 percent Korean. But all racial statistics in Hawaii are complicated and misleading. Besides, they are constantly changing. It is easy to get confused unless one keeps a few fundamental facts in mind.

One is that a majority of Hawaii's people are Oriental in origin, about 53 percent according to the figures I have used — and higher still by other estimates. Another is that all the Orientals and some of the Caucasians originally came to Hawaii as immigrant plantation laborers. They worked hard and determined that their children should do better. They put a premium on education and economic advancement. As a result, many of the people of Hawaii have the drive and vigor of a previously submerged population now coming into its own.

A Japanese *bon* dance

Still another fact, and one which disarranges all the statistics, is the high rate of intermarriage; more than one out of every three marriages in Hawaii is between members of different national or racial groups. This accounts for the fastest growing group in Hawaii, the part-Hawaiians. But, of course, they are also part-Japanese or Chinese or Caucasians. I met an Irish-Japanese-Hawaiian-Chinese hotel owner, and a German-Portuguese-Hawaiian cab-driver. Where do the statistics put them? In the part-Hawaiian category. But the point is that the statistics are becoming meaningless. In a few generations most of the people of Hawaii will be thoroughly intermingled, making efforts at precise classification futile.

The terms we use are also misleading. I have been talking about Japanese or Chinese or Portuguese or Filipinos. They are, of course, Americans of Japanese or Chinese or Portuguese or Filipino ancestry. I use the shorter terms for convenience. Besides, it would get us hopelessly involved to talk about Chinese-Negro-Hawaiian-Americans or Americans of Irish-Portuguese-Japanese ancestry. Anyway, most people in Hawaii are rather unself-conscious about all this and won't mind if descriptions of individuals or of groups are not strictly precise. But they are usually proud to list all the strains in their ancestry, and the more the better.

Hawaii is a human laboratory where old myths and prejudices are constantly being broken down. Who says that East and West can't meet? They do all the time in Hawaii.

Hawaii's multiracial, multicolored people have demonstrated the ability to get along as civilized human beings. They have had their tugs and pulls, their frictions and resentments. But they live together. They work together. They vote for each other. They mix socially. They intermarry. They respect each other's customs and traditions and religions.

Sometimes they refer to this attitude they have to each other and to visitors from the mainland as "the aloha spirit," using the word which is now the official name of the new state – Hawaii, the aloha state. It is a word which means many things. It is a word of greeting, meaning both hello and good-bye. But it also means love and affection and warmth, tolerance and understanding.

As Hawaii became a state, it was unique in the co-operation of its peoples, in the blending of its cultures, in its vigorously functioning interracial democracy. You get a feeling of this uniqueness almost everywhere in Hawaii, even in the legislature – which in so many mainland states remains a dull and routine assemblage.

Hawaiian leis are a favorite symbol of the aloha spirit, a gesture of affection for departing and arriving visitors

Imagine the scene at Iolani Palace, seat of Hawaii's state government, in May 1959 when the last territorial legislature was concluding its sessions. Here is a stately European-style edifice built in the 1880's for Hawaiian royalty – and now used by the democratic government of one of the United States, by an American legislature which includes far more Orientals than white Caucasians.

The House of Representatives is meeting in the throne room of the Palace. In front of the large chamber is the slightly faded royal red canopy under which once stood the thrones of the kings and queens of a bygone era. Still hanging from the tall ceiling are the massive crystal chandeliers brought back by King Kalakaua from Europe. On the wall hang two flags – the American flag and the Hawaiian flag with its modification of the

Iolani Palace as it looked in 1882 when it was used by Hawaiian royalty – it remains virtually unchanged

British Union Jack (a remnant of the days when Britain hoped to include Hawaii in its empire) and eight stripes for the major islands of the Hawaiian chain.

It is a warm, balmy evening. The legislature is meeting late because of the press of business; there is a lot to do to get Hawaii ready for statehood. Sitting in the chamber are legislators from all the different nationalities that make up Hawaii. They are dressed in light business suits. In the back of the room are dark-skinned Hawaiian women in muumuus, and chic Caucasian club-women out in force to stop bills to legalize horse-race betting and to ease restrictions on liquor licenses. Here are union men in bright aloha shirts lobbying for labor legislation, and nattily dressed representatives of pineapple and sugar and other business interests.

The lobbyists and spectators are restless. Every once in a while

Schooner off Diamond Head

they step out on the lanai, or porch, back of the open doors of the throne room to smoke a cigarette or talk. There is a little muttering about the "missionary influence" that is blocking the horse-racing and liquor bills. The breeze moves softly through the palm trees and banyans and kukui trees surrounding the Palace.

But inside the chamber the pace is fast, speeches short, votes frequent. Papers and notes are handed to legislators not by a page boy but by a strikingly beautiful young woman in a long white dress which somehow seems Oriental; her skin is olive, her features neither quite Caucasian nor yet Asian.

The lobbyists have to dash back for a roll call, marking off the names on long printed slips as the clerk reads them off — Japanese-sounding names like Sakae Amano, Yasutaka Fukushima, and Yoshito Takamine; Anglo-Saxon names like Roy F.

Waikiki Beach scene

Adams, Thomas P. Gill, and J. Ward Russell; Filipino names like Bernaldo Bicoy and Pedro Dela Cruz; Chinese names like Robert Wae Ching and Wadsworth Yee; Irish names like David McClung and John Milligan.

This is Hawaii, as Americans of a dozen different nationalities deal with problems of labor legislation, taxes, land reform, grapple with the new problems of statehood in an old royal palace. This is the Hawaii which elected a one-armed Japanese-American veteran of World War II, Daniel K. Inouye, to the United States Congress on the same day that a school board in Virginia, near the nation's capital, refused to hire a fully qualified school teacher because she is of Japanese ancestry. It is the Hawaii which furnishes a demonstration to the world, and a badly needed one, that American democracy does not have a "for-whites-only" sign around it. Hawaii is the best exhibit the United States has to offer the colored peoples of Asia and Africa that our country does provide equality and opportunity to people of darker skin.

Scene on Waikiki Beach

It is perhaps odd that Hawaii, our most glamorous and advertised tourist attraction, our Paradise of the Pacific, should also loom large in the serious discussions of our statesmen and politicians about international affairs. But this is surely one of the most exciting and attractivc things about Hawaii, that it is a fleet of South Sea islands which has come to terms with the twentieth century and even has something to show the rest of us Americans when it comes to modern and civilized living.

2. *Lono and the Vikings*

A dark-skinned Hawaiian lawyer sits in his office in downtown Honolulu and talks of the history of his people. Clients fill the seats in the waiting room. There is a big woman in a flowing muumuu, a defendant in a child custody case. A representative of a group of Hawaiian homesteaders on Molokai waits to present their grievance against the pineapple companies which control most of the land on the island.

"My boy comes home from school," the lawyer says, "and he wants to know about the Vikings. His teacher keeps telling the class about the Norse sailors and the open boats they used to sail across the Atlantic. Why don't they teach our kids about the Vikings of the Pacific? Why don't they tell my son that his ancestors were the greatest sailors and explorers in the world?"

The lawyer feels that the Hawaiians have been pushed aside by history, their heritage ignored, their contributions minimized. Much has been done in recent years to give the Hawaiians and the other citizens of the new state a sense of the past, more knowledge about the people who fished the sea and tilled the soil of the green islands long before the white men came. But a feeling of grievance and of frustration remains.

When Captain James Cook discovered the island of Kauai in 1778 while he was looking for the northwest passage between

Hawaiian war canoe

Europe and Asia, there had been living there for more than a thousand years a big, handsome, brown-skinned people.

Who were they? And how did they get there? The prevailing theory is that they came in the clouded dawn of prehistory from the interior of Asia, originally a Caucasian people who intermarried with the darker Malayans and Mongolians. It is believed that they were forced by the pressures of population to start island-hopping across the Pacific in search of living space of their own. They settled in Tahiti, in New Zealand, in all the islands of what is called the Polynesian triangle.

A thousand years ago, perhaps longer, a few nameless explorers from Tahiti must have found the islands of Hawaii. The new lands looked good, and soon whole families began coming 2,500 miles across the Pacific. They came in great waves, these Vikings of the Sunrise, as they have been called. They came in their big double canoes, forerunners of the speedy catamarans of today,

Interior of a grass hut as it looked in the late nineteenth century

which were capable of carrying 60 to 100 people and much cargo. They built shelters against the wind and rain on the floor between the hulls. They came with pigs and dogs and fowl, with implements of stone and wooden calabashes.

Then suddenly the migration from Tahiti stopped. The Polynesians on Hawaii remained great sailors, taking frequent voyages around their islands in outrigger canoes they hollowed out with stone tools from the trunks of trees. But for centuries they lived isolated from the world. Their ways remained the same during the centuries in which feudal Europe was transformed by the industrial revolution and America was settled and achieved independence. The ancient tools and implements which, anthropologists say, date back a thousand years are essentially the same as those found by Captain Cook. For the Hawaiians time stood still.

Legend and a general tradition to the contrary, they were not an indolent or lazy people forever lolling under the palm trees. It is true that they loved the trees and the waters and the mountains of their native islands and they enjoyed life. They played many

An old Hawaiian making poi

games, surf-riding on carved boards, coasting down steep hills on narrow sleds and sometimes just on ti leaves or coconut fronds. They had their own forms of boxing, wrestling, foot racing, bowling, even a kind of checker game. They had their fabled hulas – both a religious ceremony and an entertainment in which the graceful motions of the hands transmitted ancient tales from generation to generation. But they also worked hard.

They were great fishermen, sometimes making fish ponds in which they bred fish for easy catching. They cut trees with crude stone axes, hollowing great logs for their outrigger canoes, making calabashes from which to eat, building their houses of timber and covering them with grass – the famous grass huts long since gone except in replica as tourist attractions.

Above all, they were impressive farmers. An early explorer commented on "the indefatigable labor in making these little fields in so rugged a situation." They grew taro in raised beds like rice fields. They irrigated the fields, often through underground tunnels. From the taro they pounded a thick paste they mixed with water and called poi. Fish and poi were their principal foods. They also grew yams, breadfruit, and sugar cane. They also had pigs, dogs, and chickens which they raised and ate.

While the men fished and farmed, the women made mats and clothing from tapa, the bark of the mulberry tree, which was soaked in water and then beaten into strips. The tapa cloth was colored with dyes made from fruit juices and nuts, and designs were stamped on it with bamboo sticks. The women played a major role in society, and were often chieftainesses of equal rank with the most powerful of the males.

Perhaps the outstanding craftsmanship of the Hawaiians was in the feather cloaks and helmets made from the plumage of thousands of small birds. Specially trained trappers caught the birds; only a few choice feathers were plucked, then the birds were released.

The Hawaiians had no written language, but they had a rich vocabulary of more than 20,000 words and a considerable literature of stories, chants, genealogies, and biographies which were handed down by word of mouth. It is a soft musical language in which the vowel sounds are dominant, every syllable ending in a vowel.

There were two sharply defined social classes — the chieftain class and the common people. The land belonged to the principal chief or king on each island who in turn divided it up among the lesser chiefs. Finally, small plots were made available to the common people who had to turn over a certain share of their crops to the chiefs and to furnish labor and military service. The similarities with Western feudalism are there, but they are perhaps overstressed by applying terms such as kings and nobles to a more primitive tribal society.

Distinctions between the classes as well as between the sacred and the profane and between male and female were enforced by a rigid and intricate system of taboos called kapus. A common person could not stand in the presence of a king or touch his person. Certain foods were prohibited to women, and they could not eat with men. Violations were punished by death.

The religion was essentially a form of nature worship, and

Drawing of the heiau, or temple, at the City of Refuge on the Kona coast of the island of Hawaii, where fugitives were traditionally able to find sanctuary

every Hawaiian activity, whether building a house or launching a canoe, was inaugurated with a religious ceremony. Kane was the god of light, Lono the god of harvest, Ku the god of war, Pele the fire goddess of the volcanoes, and Kaneloa the ruler of the departed spirits.

It was Captain Cook's good fortune at first, and later his misfortune, that he was taken for Lono. Perhaps it was because he came at the harvest season or because the sails of his ship reminded the Hawaiians of the banners hung from the images of Lono. An old Hawaiian account tells of their wonder when they saw his ship:

> "It was at Waimea, on Kauai, that Lono first arrived. One said to another, 'What is that great thing with branches?' Others said, 'It is a forest that has slid down into the sea,' and the gabble

The Hawaiians bringing gifts to Captain Cook as shown in an old print

and noise was great. Then the chiefs ordered some natives to go in a canoe and observe and examine well that wonderful thing."

Cook traded nails and other iron articles for fish and food. The Hawaiians were as much amazed by the iron, something they had never seen before, as they were by Lono's appearance and by his ships. Whenever Cook went ashore, the people prostrated themselves before him. Everywhere he was greeted as Lono and the hospitable Hawaiians offered their young women to the strangers – or Haoles. Cook's first visit was not without incident. One of his officers shot an Hawaiian who grabbed for a boat hook. But he sailed away peacefully enough with his two ships, the *Resolution* and the *Discovery*.

When he returned the following year, he was again greeted as Lono by great throngs and given feather cloaks by the kings. This time, off the Kona coast of the Big Island, there were more incidents. But again Cook sailed away, only to be forced back by a heavy storm. This time the difficulties were more serious. The Hawaiians had no sense of private property. When they liked something, they took it or borrowed it. This annoyed the British sailors.

When the large cutter of the *Discovery* was stolen, Cook decided to take King Kalaniopuu of Hawaii aboard ship as a hostage. The king agreed, but one of his wives and several of his chiefs were alarmed by the conduct of Lono and his armed guards. He hesitated. A crowd gathered. There was pushing, then fighting. Cook fired and killed a man. He was struck down by the crowd. According to the Hawaiian version of the story, a chief tried to help him up. But Cook struggled to free himself and groaned. A cry went up, "He groans – he is not a god." And the people killed him.

So it was that two cultures met in Hawaii more than a century and a half ago, the culture of the West and the culture of a primitive Polynesian people. If that first meeting ended in tragedy for Captain Cook, it was but the opening scene of a greater tragedy for the Hawaiian people.

It is doubtful that Hawaii has ever been the Polynesian Garden of Eden that is sometimes pictured. There were human sacrifices in the heiaus, or temples. There were bloody wars between the chiefs of the different islands. The chiefs were often cruel, and the lot of the common people hard. But unknown to the Hawaiians were the scourges brought by the white men as well as the wonders of Western civilization.

For a few years after Captain Cook, no other white men came. Soon thereafter, however, other ships were stopping at the Sandwich Islands, as Cook had called them after a British earl. There came British, French, American, and even Russian ships. There came ships loaded with furs for China, stopping for supplies on the long voyage from the northwest American coast, and there came Yankee whaling vessels from New England. The sailors were offered food and flowers and the kindness of Hawaiian women. In return they gave many wondrous things, including trinkets, clothes, iron, seeds. Captain George Vancouver, the British explorer who was with Cook and returned three times,

An old print depicting the death of Captain Cook

brought livestock, including a bull and a cow. They also brought firearms and rum – and venereal diseases.

Indeed, the latter had already come with Cook. He marveled on his second trip how quickly it had traveled through the islands in only a few months. Venereal disease turned out to be the greatest scourge which ever befell the Hawaiian Islands. "It is not too much to say that it saturated the whole race," wrote one student. It killed off thousands. It reduced the birth rate. By undermining their resistance it made the Hawaiians susceptible to tuberculosis, smallpox, and other white men's diseases; it left them vulnerable even to measles and other minor illnesses. It sapped the vitality and strength of one of the world's handsomest and strongest peoples.

Perhaps as destructive – though not in the same sense – was the sudden introduction of the white men's values and social institutions. Greed and individual accumulation were unknown to the Hawaiians. Private property had no meaning to them. Theirs was a subsistence economy. Cook observed that they left not only their land but also their houses, hogs, and cloth "unguarded without the slightest apprehension." But then the sailors stopping over in Hawaii discovered there was a rich market in China for Hawaiian sandalwood which was used for burning incense and for fine cabinetwork. And the chiefs discovered the possibilities of wealth.

At first the chiefs were content to take beads and mirrors and other trinkets for their sandalwood. But soon they found that sandalwood could command as much as $150 a ton. Their appetites expanded and their tastes became sophisticated. In the early 1820's, one of the Hawaiian kings, Liholiho, even got a $50,000 yacht, considered the most luxurious of its time, in return for sandalwood.

Whole villages – men, women, and children – were conscripted by their chiefs to cut down the precious trees. Hillsides were denuded. Agriculture was neglected, and the people went hungry. A nineteenth-century historian noted that, according to the Hawaiians, "the chiefs left caring for their people. Their attention was turned to themselves and their immediate aggrandizement. The people became more oppressed than ever in ancient times."

In the early years of the nineteenth century foreigners of many nationalities started coming to Hawaii and settled there permanently – merchants, traders, sailors from the British ships and Yankee whaling vessels. There were Frenchmen, Portuguese, Spaniards, Italians, Chinese, even a Negro. They became important advisers to the kings. They discovered that the land was fertile, and they started accumulating substantial chunks of it in light-hearted gifts from Hawaiian kings and nobles.

In fact, it is rather remarkable, considering the rapid growth of foreign influence and the undermining of the Hawaiians' health and social institutions, that Hawaii remained at least nominally independent until annexation by the United States in 1898. Hawaii's distance from the principal centers of world power was probably the major reason. But a contributing factor was the formation, soon after the coming of the Haoles, or strangers, of a kingdom which united the principal islands.

This was the achievement of Kamehameha I, founder of a line

Baptism of an Hawaiian dignitary aboard a French ship as shown in a contemporary drawing by Jacques Arago

which lasted for eighty years and of a monarchy which endured for close to a century. The separate kingdoms which had existed hitherto would most likely have succumbed sooner. A unified monarchy reigning over all the islands was able to exert more leverage in dealing with the various foreign intruders.

Kamehameha has often been called the Napoleon of the Pacific. Whether intended as a compliment or not, the description is exaggerated. He was the product of a primitive society, of the limitations of its time and place in history, of its generosities and its cruelties.

A charming story is told of how he evolved one of his laws. During one of his civil wars, he jumped out of a canoe to attack an unoffending group of fishermen. But he slipped and caught his foot in a volcanic crevice. A fisherman, yielding to the inviting opportunity, smacked Kamehameha on the head, breaking his paddle in the process. When the fishermen were brought before

King Kamehameha I – 1737?-1819

the king for judgment, he admitted that his attack had been unjust. He decreed "The Law of the Splintered Paddle" which stated: "Let the aged, men and women, and little children lie down in safety in the road." But there is also the story of a rival chieftain who was induced to parley with Kamehameha – and who was slaughtered together with all his warriors. To keep the people of Oahu from rebelling against him he once killed all their pigs.

Beginning in 1782 as a chieftain on the Big Island, he gradually extended his sway in a series of wars of conquest. He was shrewd enough to employ the services of several Haole retainers and advisers and to concentrate in his possession an arsenal of white men's weapons which by 1804 consisted of 600 muskets, 14 small cannon, and some 20 armed sailing vessels. An independent kingdom on Kauai gave him trouble for some years. But at his death in 1819 he had for more than two decades been the undisputed overlord of the Hawaiian chain.

Kamehameha realized that a direct challenge to the rising power of the Western nations in the islands was impossible. So he sought to bargain, and at times to play off rival claimants against one another. He offered in 1794 to cede the Big Island to Britain – in return for a promise that its religion, government, and customs would remain intact. Although the British rejected the agreement, the islands did come under British influence for many years. He accepted the British Union Jack as the flag of Hawaii. But when the Americans reportedly protested during the War of 1812, he agreed to combine the British emblem with eight American-style stripes for the islands of Hawaii.

When he discovered that Hawaiian sandalwood cargoes were required to pay duty in Chinese ports, he quickly realized the revenue-producing possibilities for his kingdom and imposed duties of his own. Without too much trouble, he disposed of a Russian scheme to take over the islands instituted by Dr. George Scheffer, a German adventurer and physician. When Scheffer ingratiated himself with the king of Kauai, Kamehameha ordered his expulsion and the Russian dream of empire ended ingloriously in 1817.

Although he was hospitable to the Westerners, Kamehameha was also somewhat wary of them. The Hawaiians were never hostile to the Haoles in their midst, but some of them began to worry. A British missionary observed later that some Hawaiians "said they had heard that in several countries where foreigners had intermingled with the original natives, the latter soon disappeared."

Kamehameha has become the symbol of the old Hawaii before the coming of the Haoles. He retained the old kapu customs and the old religion, maintaining the heiaus, or temples, intact and building new ones, preserving the independence of his kingdom. But actually the ravages of disease and of greed had already begun to take their toll during his reign. The people of the islands were dying off. Kamehameha himself almost died in a plague which killed most of his chiefs. And in his lifetime Honolulu was becoming a wide-open, booming seaport, its harbor a forest of sails and its streets full of sailors looking for girls and liquor.

Hawaii has since been the scene of a happy blending of cultures and peoples. But it was not so in the beginning. It was not only Western disease which was fatal to the Hawaiians. It was a way of life which was totally different from their own and which was bound to triumph in the end. A wise Hawaiian woman, whose mother was Hawaiian, her father Caucasian, tried to sum up the difference for me:

> "My mother's people would look at the sunrise and say how beautiful it is. They would sit and fish and look at the sun and enjoy it. My father's people would look at the sun and ask: How far is it and how much does it weigh?"

3. *New England in Polynesia*

Reverend Hiram Bingham, who came to Hawaii from New England in 1820 burning with zeal to convert the natives, was not a man to let small obstacles stand in his way. He was a man of enormous energy, determination, and faith. Yet sometimes he had grim forebodings of the magnitude of his task and pondered on "the deep pagan gloom" which engulfed the Hawaiians.

Once Bingham saw some hula dancers cast their leis into a small enclosure sacred to the god of the hula-hula. He described in his journal how he catechized them:

> "Does the god of the hula-hula know anything?"
> "No."
> "Can he see?"
> "No."
> "Can he hear?"
> "No."
> "Can he speak?"
> "No."
> "Can he do anything?"
> "No."
> "What is he good for? And why do you have such a god?"
> "For play," they answered.

It was an answer, as Bradford Smith suggests in *Yankees in Paradise,* that was to remain forever alien to Bingham and

A British traveler gave this impression of early missionary efforts

his associates. Between the missionaries and the Hawaiians there was a chasm in temperaments, ways of life, and sexual mores that was never really bridged. Monogamy and marriage in the Western sense were unknown to the Hawaiians.

There was perhaps never a more unlikely meeting of peoples than between the stern and fervent Yankee missionaries and the carefree Hawaiians. Yet their impact on Hawaii was lasting and profound and their role is still a subject of lively controversy. The missionaries were not only the agents of Protestantism in Hawaii. They were also the bearers of American influence and culture, of American economic and political control, and they are sometimes blamed for the destruction of the old ways and the old life. Actually, the disintegration of Hawaiian society started well before the missionaries landed. It was rather their role to accelerate processes already well under way and to try to shape a dying way of life into a new mold by offering an alternative set of ideals and form of organization.

In fact, their early successes were due in part to the breakup of the system of kapu, or religious prohibitions, on the eve of their arrival. King Liholiho, Kamehameha's successor, abolished the kapus in 1819, responding both to general Western influence and to pressure from the chieftainesses who wanted an end to some of the discriminations enforced by the old ways.

There is a touching story which traces the beginnings of the Protestant mission to a young Hawaiian named Opukahaia who had been brought to New Haven, Connecticut, by a Yankee sea captain. One day he was found weeping on the steps of Yale College because he was ignorant and uneducated. Soon he was converted and taught Christian ways. Opukahaia's story inspired the newly created American Board of Commissioners for Foreign Missions, a nondenominational body made up mainly of Congregationalists and Presbyterians, to send a mission to Hawaii. Reverend Hiram Bingham, Reverend Asa Thurston, and several others volunteered their services. Opukahaia died of typhus shortly before the mission sailed on the vessel *Thaddeus*. But aboard were four young Hawaiians who had been trained at a mission school in Connecticut.

It was these young Hawaiians, sent ashore at Kailua on the Big Island, who brought back the good news that the new king had burned the idols and destroyed the temples.

The missionaries had come at a most propitious time. The old kapus were dead, and the Hawaiians were ready for the new kapus brought by the Haoles.

The Haoles with their long necks and strange clothes were well received. The king's prime minister and other dignitaries came aboard the *Thaddeus* with their ladies. They thought that the women in the party looked thin and scrawny. One buxom, high-born Hawaiian dandled a missionary wife on her ample lap and advised her to eat and grow fat. But the fact that the missionaries had brought their women and children was a count in their favor, proving their peaceful intentions.

It was hard for the missionaries at first, especially for the women. Setting up the kind of homes to which they were accustomed took time. Liholiho was friendly, in a stand-offish fashion. He even agreed to become converted himself — if he could have a five-year moratorium in which to sin with his many wives. But his chiefs were suspicious and the sailors, sea captains, and traders of all nationalities were hostile. The missionaries were forever inveighing against the easy sexual relations

Temperance Advocate,

AND SEAMEN'S FRIEND.

HONOLULU, OAHU, SANDWICH ISLANDS, SEPT. 16, 1843.

SEAMEN'S CHAPEL, Honolulu, Oahu.

The missionaries sought to inculcate temperance among the seamen as this newspaper indicates

between the sailors and the Hawaiian women. Moreover, they sought to curb the profitable trade in rum – even in tobacco.

But the missionaries were determined, and they worked hard. They learned Hawaiian quickly, systematized an Hawaiian alphabet, set up printing presses, printed the Bible in Hawaiian. Liholiho let them educate his chiefs; he drew the line at educating the commoners who were needed to chop down sandalwood. Soon the missionaries were setting up schools for Hawaiian children, but kept their own children apart lest they be contaminated by the "lewdness" of the Hawaiians, meaning their uninhibited sexual mores. The missionary wives were helpful and influential; and their skill with the needle was a valuable asset. The chieftainesses and other high-born women were most anxious to wear the long gowns sewn by the missionary wives, and some of them became zealous converts.

Kapiolani, an important chieftainess, made a daring demonstration of her faith in 1824. With one of the missionaries and about eighty followers, she climbed to the rim of the great crater of Kilauea, the home of Pele, the volcano goddess. There she proclaimed her faith in Jehovah and defied Pele to do her worst. When Kapiolani was not engulfed by hot lava, the assembled company sang a hymn of praise. The turning point seems to have come when Kaahumanu, one of the wives of Kamehameha and a regent under two of his successors, became a convert. She liked to hold the lady missionaries affectionately on her lap. When she died clutching a copy of the New Testament, this was a powerful argument for the new faith.

Soon the missionaries were converting the Hawaiians by the hundreds and the thousands. Reverend Bingham preached in an improvised Honolulu tabernacle to crowds of 2,000. Reverend Titus Coan, a fire-eating revivalist preacher, attracted huge throngs on the Big Island. When a village was wiped out by an eruption on the Big Island, he blamed it on the sinfulness of the inhabitants. In sixty years more than 70,000 were converted.

The missionaries were sometimes troubled by the knowledge that the Hawaiians were dying off faster than they were being brought to Christianity. Venereal and other diseases were continuing to take their toll. It is estimated that there were 300,000 islanders in Captain Cook's time. By 1853 the first formal census counted only 71,000. But whatever their private misgivings, the missionaries never questioned their success publicly. Reverend Henry T. Cheever said that the triumph of the mission "will be none the less real and true though, in the mysterious providence of God, the whole native race expire just as it is Christianized."

Of course, the missionaries were not responsible for the extinction of the Hawaiians. Indeed, their contributions in introducing modern medicine were notable. They had many other achievements to their credit. They performed miracles in education, gradually making most of the Hawaiians literate. But the fact remained that the Hawaiians were dying – and that the introduction of Western civilization with both its virtues and vices was fatal to their way of life.

The missionaries could not separate their religious faith from

An old photo of the settlement for victims of leprosy on Molokai

their other values or even from their customs. They sought to impose their whole civilization, and all at once. They replaced the skimpy native garments with Mother Hubbards, which later became the colorful muumuus. The wife of the missionary doctor taught the women to make cake and bread and pie which must have seemed to her more Christian than poi. The laws they sponsored sought to regulate a moral behavior which was strikingly different from their own. More than half the Hawaiians involved in police cases in Honolulu in 1846 were charged with adultery or fornication.

Perhaps because they were so rigid in their demands, the missionaries were always confronted with backsliding among their converts both of high and low degree. Inflexibly they tried to make the Hawaiians into New England Yankees, and the attempt was bound to fail. The churches they founded declined in membership from 24,000 in 1856 to 4,628 in 1898, a drop not altogether accounted for by loss in population. The Catholics,

A whaling vessel in Honolulu, around 1863

Mormons, and other creeds, more flexible in their approach, made greater headway. It is, in fact, one of the tragedies of the missionaries that their greatest impact was not so much spiritual as political and economic.

Their view of government was theocratic, much like that of the early Puritans. Reverend Bingham said that the state "ought to be, and in an important sense is, a religious institution." Within a generation, five members of the mission resigned to become important advisers to the Kamehameha dynasty. They used their posts to combat the influence of the French Catholic missionaries who became active in the 1830's – and also of French and British efforts to win Hawaii for their empires. It seemed only right to them that the monarchy should be steered toward ever closer contact with the United States.

The most important reform they introduced, and one still bitterly resented by many Hawaiians, was the Great Mahele, or land division of 1848. The missionaries proposed this measure with the best of intentions – making more land available to the common people. As they reported to headquarters in Boston, they sought "to encourage habits of industry" as well as "punctuality in all engagements, especially the payment of debts." What was more natural than that they should see a vision of the Hawaiians as industrious small farmers, New England-style?

So they proposed that some 28,000 acres be divided among the common people. While this does not seem like very much, it included some of Hawaii's best agricultural land. Far larger, although generally poorer, areas were allocated to the king, to the government, and to the chiefs. For a people accustomed to private ownership of land, the Mahele would have been a boon. But in Hawaii, where private property had never been an established or accepted institution, it opened the way for the alienation of the Hawaiians from their land. It marked the end of the old system under which all the land was under the guardianship of the king – and the beginning of large-scale private ownership of land by the white-skinned Haoles from across the sea.

Even before the Great Mahele, plantations had been started by enterprising foreigners. But it was the Mahele that paved the way for rapid growth of plantations all over the islands. The planters bought up the land made available to the commoners for a few cents an acre, and before long they were reaching out for the land of the chiefs and the government.

In 1850 the *Honolulu Times,* a short-lived anti-mission weekly, printed a letter asking how to acquire land in the islands. The editor's comment was caustic: "Go to Boston and be appointed a missionary." Thus the belief early gained currency that the missionaries were hypocritical land-grabbers. And the old question began to be propounded: "Did they do good – or did they do well?"

There were many foreigners who got land at the time, missionaries among them. In 1852 there were 16 missionaries who held title to 7,886 acres – and 20 who had acquired no land. Most successful of the missionaries turned businessmen were Amos Cooke and Samuel Castle. Released from the mission to handle its financial affairs, they formed Castle & Cooke in 1851, which later became one of the controlling sugar companies in Hawaii. On the first day of his new career, Cooke wrote in his diary:

> "The foreigners are creeping in among the natives, getting their largest and best lands, water privileges, building lots, etc. The Lord seems to be allowing such things to take place that the Islands may gradually pass into other hands. . . . Our large plain of sand is now covered with vegetation and is laid out into lots. I am proposing, ere long, to purchase some of them. . . ."

Perhaps among some there was a lessening of the early zeal. There were complaints in reports back home about the "worldliness" spreading among the brethren. It was a time when the mission was cutting loose from Boston, and many were casting about for independent sources of income. The older missionaries were retiring. The younger generation was going into business and agriculture, and in most cases the business firms associated with the missionary families were founded by the missionaries' sons or other relatives. But on the whole, the missionaries saw no wrongdoing in their acquisitions; nor would they have frowned on those of their descendants. Thrift and enterprise were part of their way of life. Some of the missionary families became wealthy; others did not. It should be realized also that many others besides missionaries and their descendants went into business in Hawaii. Among the founders of great fortunes were sailors, sea captains, and merchants who for many years bitterly fought the missionaries.

A half-page advertisement in a recent statehood edition of one of the Honolulu newspapers put the case for the missionaries. The ad, inserted by The Hawaiian Evangelical Association of Congregational Christian Churches, which is a direct outgrowth of early missionary efforts, said:

> "There is no doubt in the minds of many historians and writers that this group of missionaries and their followers exerted such an influence for righteousness, justice and the good of all the

King William C. Lunalilo

King David Kalakaua

people that they were one of the most potent forces for the development of an orderly government. . . . They led the way down the path that has ultimately led us to Statehood."

But a dark-skinned Hawaiian driver and tourist-guide, showing a few of us around the Big Island, takes a sharply contradictory view. Pointing to an old church, its neat white spire somehow incongruous in the midst of the bright tropical foliage, he rattles off his spiel:

"The missionaries came to Hawaii in 1820. They converted the Hawaiians to Christianity. The Hawaiians took the Bible and they went out and preached, and the missionaries took the land."

We have been laughing at most of our guide's comments, and we laugh at this one too. But there is a shade of embarrassment in our laughter, for frequent repetition and deliberate drollery have not completely dulled the edge of his words.

After all these years, the historical role of the missionaries is still one of Hawaii's liveliest controversial issues – a complex issue in which there are rights and wrongs on both sides.

Foreigners had been prominent in the Hawaiian monarchy well before the Mahele and the rise of the sugar plantations. But now their stake in government increased. They needed laborers for their plantations – and they wanted the government to import them. They also needed a market for their sugar, especially in the United States. American merchants and missionaries and their sons began to dominate the cabinets of the monarchy and to play the role of king-makers.

After the death of the last of the Kamehameha dynasty in 1872, the legislature was convened to pick the king. It was charged that William Charles Lunalilo, the successful candidate, was the American choice over David Kalakaua. In any case, all but one of the members of Lunalilo's cabinet were Americans. His foreign minister was Charles Reed Bishop, founder of the Bishop National Bank. But Lunalilo lasted only a year, and this time it was Kalakaua who was said to have American support over the Dowager Queen Emma. Hawaiians took to the streets in protest demonstrations and riots, and British and American marines were landed in Honolulu to maintain Kalakaua's crown.

Seemingly, Kalakaua paid off his Haole supporters by negotiating the first reciprocity treaty with the United States in 1876. Hawaiian sugar was to have favored treatment in the American market – in return for similar treatment for American products, plus a guarantee that Hawaii would not cede Pearl Harbor or any other port or territory to any other nation. Reciprocity has been described as the "wonder-worker" of Hawaiian sugar. Within twenty years after the treaty, sugar production increased by ten times.

Yet Kalakaua turned out to be a disappointment, particularly to the missionary element. A big, convivial fellow, he won a reputation as a heavy drinker despite his early education at the missionary school for chiefs. Robert Louis Stevenson, who was fond of him, wrote that he carried his drink "like a mountain with a sparrow on its shoulders." He enjoyed a game of cards, and the story is told how once, playing with the sugar magnate Claus Spreckels, he said "I have five kings," putting down his hand with four kings and pointing to himself as the fifth. He

King Kalakaua with Robert Louis Stevenson

staged a lavish coronation, rivaling that of any European monarch, got himself and his queen expensive jeweled crowns, and bought himself an up-to-date $20,000 battery of European guns. His expenses were lavish, and he sponsored schemes for a government-financed lottery and for an opium monopoly to raise revenue.

Some of his doings, while apparently even more ludicrous, had a serious undercurrent. At one time he conceived the idea of marrying an Hawaiian princess to a Japanese prince so as to effect an alliance between the two monarchies. His, too, was a short-lived "primacy of the Pacific" program whereby Hawaii was going to take over Tonga, Samoa, and other still unclaimed islands. He even sent an ill-fated little makeshift battleship to Samoa to promote his plan; it just barely limped back to port in Honolulu.

Behind some of these antics was a latent nationalism, the desperate floundering of a people who feared extinction. The slogan "Hawaii for Hawaiians" was raised in little newspapers, and at meetings of new secret societies. Ancient rites were increasingly

A luau in the latter days of the monarchy

observed, and offerings were left at the old heiaus. Kalakaua sponsored a native fraternal order which attempted to preserve ancient Hawaiian beliefs and values.

The Hawaiian monarchy, for all its tarnished glory, its comic-opera aspects, its lack of real power, became a symbol to the Hawaiians of their last hope to retain their independence. And many Hawaiians, liberal and democratic in other respects, look back with nostalgia and fondness on the monarchy as the time of an Hawaii still ruled by Hawaiians, of a proud time that is past and will never return.

Kalakaua's was a gay reign, and many still regard it as Hawaii's golden era. There were glittering parties at the palace, which even the missionaries attended. Honolulu blossomed as a modern city, with horse- and mule-drawn streetcars, a telephone system, an opera house. But underneath all the display there was mounting tension between the Hawaiians and the Haoles.

A mule-drawn car in Honolulu during Kalakaua's reign

When the United States Senate refused to renew the sugar reciprocity treaty unless the United States got exclusive rights to Pearl Harbor as a naval base, Kalakaua balked. So in 1887 a Haole-backed palace revolution ousted Walter Murray Gibson, the anti-mission American adviser considered responsible for the king's unco-operative attitude. There was also forced on Kalakaua a new constitution limiting his powers in favor of his Haole cabinet.

When Kalakaua died in San Francisco in 1891 on one of his numerous trips abroad, he was succeeded by his sister, Liliuokalani. Although educated by the missionaries, she was hostile to their influence. She shared, and even more single-mindedly than Kalakaua, her brother's nativist or nationalist sentiments. She was a large woman, regal in her bearing. Full of dignity, she strode only briefly across the stage of history. The end was already in sight.

King Kalakaua's funeral in 1891

The queen opposed the 1887 constitution. She wanted to rule as well as reign. But now some of the Haole businessmen, organized in what Liliuokalani angrily described as "the missionary party," were determined to get rid of the increasingly troublesome Hawaiian monarchy.

They were faced with a sharp depression, the result of the McKinley tariff of 1890 which put Hawaiian sugar at a disadvantage by giving a two-cent bounty to American sugar producers. Annexation to remove this differential became a necessity. An Annexation Club was formed by leading citizens. A militia was organized. But the government was ousted without violence.

Resistance was hopeless. The cruiser *Boston* was conveniently nearby. John L. Stevens, the United States Minister, was close to the annexationists, and arranged for the landing of American troops.

The late John H. Wilson, a part-Hawaiian who many years

Queen Liliuokalani

afterward became mayor of Honolulu, used to quip bitterly: "For two cents a pound in the price of sugar a queen beloved by her people was overthrown."

A provisional government was installed headed by Sanford B. Dole, judge of the Supreme Court of Hawaii, son of missionaries and a distant relative of the Doles who made pineapple a great Hawaiian industry.

But now there was a last-minute hitch. The provisional government was not as enthusiastically accepted in Washington as the annexationists had hoped. Grover Cleveland, who became President just at this point, looked with disfavor on the expansionist schemes then current in the capital. He appointed James H. Blount as an emissary to look into the situation. Blount heard both sides and reported that a lawful government had been overthrown by an unlawful revolution aided by the United States Minister. In a fiery message to Congress, the President declared:

> "The lawful government of Hawaii was overthrown without the drawing of a sword or the firing of a shot by a process every step of which, it may safely be asserted, is directly traceable to

President Sanford B. Dole of the Provisional Government at desk, surrounded by three of his ministers

and dependent for its success upon the agency of the United States acting through its diplomatic and naval representatives."

When it turned out that annexation would take a while, the provisional government was turned into the Republic of Hawaii with Dole as President. After an abortive royalist revolution in 1895, Liliuokalani was arrested as one of the plotters and kept a prisoner in her former royal palace. There she wrote one of the most beloved of Hawaiian songs, "Aloha Oe."

Finally, Congress approved annexation in 1898 at a time when expansionist sentiment was riding high on the wave of the Spanish-American War. Two years later President McKinley duly appointed Dole governor of the new territory. And ex-President Cleveland commented, "I am ashamed of the whole affair."

Some old people still remember those times. One of them is Jennie Wilson, who was a hula dancer in the Hawaiian court and who performed before the royalty of Europe. The widow of former Mayor Wilson and a lively eighty-seven when I saw her in 1959, she exclaimed:

Sanford Dole and his wife at their Honolulu residence

> "They didn't take the country in a good way. They took it by force. They stole it from a queen who refused to sign away the rights of her people. They made her a prisoner."

Was there a good way? Could there have been a less destructive way? Perhaps not. But this much is certain. When the Hawaiians became citizens of the United States, their plight was critical. Their population, and this included the already growing number of part-Hawaiians, was less than 40,000. The Hawaiians were a minority in their own country. They had little land. Most of them lived in poverty. If the story had ended there, it would have been the all-too-familiar tragedy of the white man's expansion into the lands of primitive peoples. While nothing that happened subsequently could altogether erase the tragedy, the story did not end. The Hawaiian people, although sadly depleted, did not wholly perish. And in one sense at least they triumphed. For the influence of their ways, their culture, and their language remains strong in Hawaii even today.

Sanford Dole inaugurated as governor of the territory of Hawaii in 1900

A Citizens Guard which supported the Dole government and helped thwart the royalist revolt of 1895

4. Sugar-Coated Fort

"When my grandfather came over as a sailor in 1866, he was told everything was all sewed up, that all the good land was already taken. But then he discovered that water could be brought up by digging deep wells. Thousands of new acres of sugar cane were brought into cultivation, and he made his fortune. Then pineapple was brought in."

Benjamin F. Dillingham, the vigorous youngish man sitting in the old-fashioned paneled office, was talking about his grandfather of the same name. Occasionally secretaries tiptoed in, called him "Mr. Ben" with affectionate deference. He is a member of one of the great Haole families which helped sweep away the monarchy and then for many years after were the new ruling group in Hawaii. The Dillingham family now has far-reaching interests in construction, transportation, coffee, cattle, real estate. It has recently undertaken major projects in the Middle East and in Latin America, and it developed a new $28-million shopping center in Honolulu.

"Hawaii's great period of development was still ahead in my grandfather's time," young Mr. Ben continues, "although nobody thought so. Well, I feel the same way today. Hawaii hasn't passed her last economic frontier yet. There are thousands of acres of lava wasteland for which new uses will be found. New businesses

The old Spreckels mansion in Honolulu – home of one of the great sugar families

will develop. New opportunities will open up."

There was, indeed, a period of dynamic growth and opportunity in the time of the elder Dillingham, and there is such a period now. But it is the period in between which is still a matter of some controversy in Hawaii. This is described variously as the period of "benevolent paternalism" or of "semi-feudalism" or of "Big Five domination." It was the period when the five major corporations in the sugar industry were the dominant force in Hawaii's economy. Sometimes the Dillingham interests are added to make a Big Sixth, perhaps even outranking some of the others.

It was a period lasting more than half a century which was summed up some years ago by Ray Stannard Baker, the prominent journalist and friend of Woodrow Wilson: "I have rarely

The English Club in 1877 – seat of British influence in Hawaii

visited any place where there was as much charity and as little democracy as in Hawaii." It was a period which lasted until World War II.

As late as August 1941, a full-length article in *Fortune* magazine described Hawaii as a "Sugar-Coated Fort." It said that the top layers of Hawaiian society were still living in the nineteenth century, while the armed forces were preparing for all-out mobilization in a twentieth-century war. "The rich Haoles stick close together, marry each other, give small parties and avoid ostentation," *Fortune* said. "The rich Haoles have something of the old-time New Englanders' stiff-necked self-righteousness; they resent innovation and dislike intrusion." It was their aim, said *Fortune*, "to keep Hawaii just the way it is."

But this is getting somewhat ahead of the story. First there was the time of old Ben Dillingham, the grandfathers and the great-grandfathers of the present generation, of hard-driving missionaries and sons of missionaries, of Yankee sea captains and whaling men, of enterprising German, Irish, British, and Norwegian immigrants. They started plantations, founded mercantile houses which made great fortunes and grew into the Big Five sugar agencies. The fortunes were made by men who came to

An early sugar mill – around 1867

Hawaii and stayed there and raised families there, not by absentee owners – as was the case in Alaska or in most of the world's colonial areas.

At first individual planters tried to market their own sugar through visiting sea captains and to order machinery and equipment on their own. But gradually the Honolulu trading firms which did business with the plantations began to take over these functions as well as to meet the constantly expanding need for capital. This was the origin of the sugar factors or agencies, of the Big Five companies which were founded between 1836 and 1851, C. Brewer & Co., Ltd., Castle & Cooke, Ltd., Alexander & Baldwin, Ltd., American Factors, Ltd., and Theo. H. Davies & Co. Ltd. The "Ltd." is a hangover from the British influence strong at that period. But only one of the five, Davies & Co., had British capital behind it. American Factors, founded by Captain Henry Hackfeld, a German trader, was backed by German capital. Hackfeld did not seem a patriotic name during World War I, and the company was reorganized under its present name. C. Brewer was started by sea captains, Castle & Cooke by mis-

Old hand method of cutting sugar cane

sionaries, Alexander & Baldwin by sons of missionaries.

With the mainland market assured as a result of reciprocity and annexation, new plantations were founded and old ones expanded. Primitive sugar mills were scrapped, bigger ones built. Fertilizers were applied to the soil in prodigious quantities, and daring men embarked on huge irrigation projects. S. T. Alexander and H. P. Baldwin got the idea of digging a great ditch on Maui to bring water from the rainy northern slope of Mount Haleakala to the dry valley where they had a small plantation. It was a tough job, and pipes had to be brought across steep ravines. When workmen refused to lower themselves by ropes down one deep gorge, Baldwin, who had already lost an arm in a mill accident, used his legs and his one good arm to lead the way.

Sugar planting soon became a big enterprise. It had to be by its very nature, requiring lots of water and fertilizer, milling, and transportation. It was an integrated operation. Factories and fields were inseparable. And the trend was toward ever larger plantations. In 1883, there were 90 plantations producing 57,000 tons of sugar. By 1939, 39 plantations were accounting for a

Spraying the cane with herbicide

million tons a year. The concentration of financial control was an inevitable by-product.

In this manner the Big Five began to manage and eventually to own the plantations. Whole groups of plantations were thus under common direction, and the entire industry was tied together through family connections, interlocking directorates, through an extremely effective industry association organized as the Planters Labor and Supply Company and now known as the Hawaiian Sugar Planters' Association (HSPA). As the industry prospered, surplus capital from sugar poured into pineapple, cattle ranching, department stores and merchandising, light and power industries, a telegraph system, and steamship lines – especially the Matson Navigation Company, which was organized by the sugar industry. Thus the Big Five mushroomed from small Honolulu trading firms into giant enterprises con-

Spidery superstructure supports irrigation flume across deep gully in sugar-cane field on the island of Hawaii

trolling and directing not only the sugar industry but most of the Hawaiian economy.

Pineapple came into the picture well after sugar. It was not until 1885 that the first pineapple plantation was started. Actually the modern pineapple industry dates from 1901 – when James Dole, a distant relative of Sanford Dole, organized the Hawaiian Pineapple Company, Ltd., still the biggest in Hawaii and in the world. A couple of years later canning of pineapple began on a commercial scale, and the industry within a few years became second only to sugar. Although two mainland companies started competitive pineapple operations, the Big Five were also a controlling influence in much of the industry.

Technically and industrially the sugar and pineapple companies and the plantations they controlled were enterprising and

Laying down mulch paper for pineapple planting

even daring. HSPA set up an experiment station, and the companies contributed generously to its support. Trained scientists discovered new varieties of cane and found methods to combat deadly parasites. When the leaf hopper many years ago threatened the entire sugar crop, scientists went to Australia and other sugar companies and found parasites which destroyed the hopper by laying eggs on its body. They imported fat pop-eyed toads from Puerto Rico which devour harmful insects. They pioneered in inventing machinery used all over the world for processing the raw sugar from cane. As early as 1901, they developed a mechanical rake which pulls the cane from cars to a traveling conveyor in the mills. Much later came the mechanical harvester which helped make the Hawaiian sugar industry the most mechanized as well as the most productive in the world. Marketing and industrial techniques were equally highly developed. The sugar companies established the world's largest sugar-refining plant in the world at Crockett, California.

The pineapple industry was similarly inventive. At first came experimentation to find the right variety of pineapple, mainly the smooth cayenne, for Hawaii's soil. Discovery of an iron sul-

Planting pineapple through a layer of mulch paper

phate spray increased production by providing the soil with necessary iron. In 1913 there was invented the ingenious machine called the Ginaca – which cuts off the ends of the pineapple and removes the shell and core in one operation, leaving a golden cylinder of fruit on the trimming table. The companies organized the Pineapple Research Institute, which has done extensive experimental work. Among many other contributions, it has developed the present method of planting pineapple through a black asphalt-treated sheet called mulch paper. Laid on the ground by machine, this paper fumigates and fertilizes at the same time. It holds the moisture in the ground, increases soil temperature, and prevents growth of weeds. Pineapple slips are planted through holes in the paper to start a new crop.

But while they were scientifically and industrially advanced, the sugar and pineapple industries lagged behind in other respects. Their tightly knit system of economic control, inhospitable to newcomers and to competitive enterprise, reminded many of

Pineapple canneries in the Iwilei section of Honolulu

feudalism. So did the paternalistic labor conditions on the plantations, which were far behind the times.

There were other grandfathers who came to Hawaii at about the same time as the elder Dillingham. I talked to some of their grandsons and granddaughters too: Japanese, Chinese, Portuguese, Filipinos, descendants of the field laborers who had been brought over in the last century to work on the sugar plantations. And for the most part they did not feel until quite recently that opportunity in Hawaii was a very meaningful thing for them or that they participated as equals in the shaping of a democratic community.

At first Hawaiians were used on the plantations. But the planters described them as "improvidential and unreliable," and complained of their natural indolence. From this grew the all-too-familiar stereotype of the Hawaiians as lazy. Actually, the Hawaiians made excellent sailors as well as fine, hard-working cowboys on the Big Island. But cutting cane under the hot sun — on land which they felt had been taken away from their people by strangers — was not their favorite pursuit. It is difficult to blame them. Some did remain on the plantations as skilled work-

A hydraulically operated mechanism starts the fruit on its way through the cannery. Fruit is graded for size as the journey begins

ers and teamsters. But there were hardly enough Hawaiians left, only about 50,000 of them in 1872 when the population of Hawaii reached an all-time low. Polynesians from the Gilbert Islands, many of them shanghaied aboard ship, were tried out by the planters; but they, too, seemed little suited for the hard plantation work.

Then the planters started importing Chinese, found them "quiet, able, and willing men." There was a complaint that they showed "a considerable disposition to hang to themselves" in their new surroundings. But they were hard-working, and did not seem to grumble much at initial wages of $3 a month. Thousands of them were brought, a total of 44,000 altogether, during the 1870's and 1880's, and their wages were gradually increased to $10 and $12 a month.

But the Chinese proved less tractable than at first they appeared to be. By 1883, the *Planters Monthly* commented, "Chinamen are cunning, and quick to perceive their advantage." The planters gradually came to the conclusion that there was "less

The Ginaca machine removes the core and shell

danger of collusion among laborers" when workers of different nationalities were employed.

Next came the turn of the Japanese. They were tried out and described as "most satisfactory." The *Planters Monthly* said the Japanese assumed "so readily the customs and habits of the country, that there does not exist the same prejudice against them that there is with the Chinese." In a few decades 140,000 Japanese were brought into Hawaii in successive waves. But the *Planters Monthly* noted "the tendency to strike and desert which their well-nigh full possession of the labor market fosters."

Workers of a dozen different nationalities were brought in to provide diversity and to assure an ample labor supply. Portuguese, Korean, Puerto Rican, German, Norwegian, Spanish, Russian, Polish, and Filipino workers were imported. Next to the

Hawaiian cowboys are paniolas – a variation on Español – after the Mexican ranch hands brought in during the last century to teach them the tricks of the trade

Japanese, the Filipinos were the largest group. About 124,000 of them were brought in altogether. From these two nationalities came the bulk of the workers imported by the planters over the years.

That was how Hawaii became a land of many peoples. Workers from all over the world were brought in as plantation labor. Many went back after a few years. But more settled down and stayed and married and had children. Hard as life was on the plantations, it was generally no worse than in Japan or China or the other countries of Asia and often it was better. But that is not saying very much.

Between the imported laborers and the Haole plantation owners and managers there was an unbridgeable gulf. The term Haole now acquired a new meaning. It no longer meant just a stranger; nor did it refer to all whites. Portuguese and Spanish

Immigrant plantation workers in the 1880's – mainly Chinese and Japanese

laborers were not Haoles. The term embraced chiefly those who were on top of the economic heap.

Workers were at first brought in under a compulsory contract system, with penal offenses for absenteeism or refusal to work. Gradually, punitive provisions were softened and tempered. But not until 1900, after Hawaii became a United States territory, was the old contract system finally abolished, and its end was hailed by a march to Honolulu by thousands of Japanese workers from neighboring plantations.

Stern labor discipline was often combined with a paternalistic attitude, especially on the plantations owned or managed by missionaries. At the Kohala plantation a set of rules posted in 1862 "requested" laborers to attend church every Sunday for prayer meeting. No laborer was allowed "to leave the Plantation by day or night" without express permission. "There is to be no card playing . . . No quarreling with or whipping wives is allowed . . . No tittle tattling is allowed."

In modified form, this type of paternalism persisted until relatively recent times. The best of the plantation managers considered themselves responsible for their employees, and in some instances there were medical and other welfare programs of a high order. But there were substantial variations in conditions. There were many brutal overseers and plantation housing on the whole ranged from inadequate to bad. Housing and other services provided by management were called "perquisites" and were considered part of the monthly wages paid the workers. The plantation was a self-contained little world controlled by its owners and managers, on whom the immigrant plantation workers were entirely dependent.

There were sporadic protests by plantation laborers against poor food or housing or against brutality by a plantation supervisor, or luna. On occasion the Chinese and Japanese Government intervened, threatening to shut off immigration unless conditions were improved.

A typical complaint was voiced by a young Japanese worker:

> "We can stand the long hours of work in the hot sun, but it burns us up to have an ignorant luna stand around and holler and swear at us all the time for not working fast enough. Another thing that gripes me is to have the lunas walk right into my house without knocking and waiting till I say 'come.' "

But the plantation workers were thousands of miles from their homelands. They did not speak English – and at first they couldn't even communicate with workers of other nationalities. Segregated into little settlements of their own on each plantation, the workers of different nationalities distrusted each other. Unions and strikes were all but impossible under such circumstances. As late as 1938, one authority wrote, "the strike is something of an anomaly within the plantation system, amounting practically to a form of treason." Yet strikes did, infrequently, take place.

In 1909, Japanese laborers on Oahu formed a Higher Wage Association which charged that they were getting $18 a month for 26 working days, while Portuguese and Puerto Ricans doing the same work were getting $22.50 plus decent housing and land on which to garden. They appealed to the planters that, since prices had gone up and the Japanese were now becoming parmanent residents in Hawaii and raising families, they needed more money.

A typical plantation worker presented an itemized budget to his employer: "Let me show you how my monthly account stands," he said, "how much a man of $18 can save each month." He figured out, after including items like seventy-five cents for laundry, twenty-five cents for baths, and five cents for haircuts, that he was left with only ten cents' savings a day.

When their plea for higher wages was turned down, they did the almost unprecedented and went out on strike. But divisions among the different nationalities defeated them. The planters offered Hawaiian, Korean, Japanese, and Portuguese laborers $1.50 a day to break the strike. The wages were so enticing that the newcomers refused to leave when the strike petered out.

The 1909 strike is credited with raising wages somewhat on the plantations. But it was a decade before there was another serious strike on the plantations. This time, in 1920, the Japanese and the Filipinos walked out at almost the same time. An appeal from the Japanese union put the case eloquently:

> "We are faithful laborers, willing to follow the steps of our departed elders and do our part toward Hawaii's production. We hear that there are in Hawaii over 100 millionaires, men chiefly connected with the sugar plantations. It is not our purpose to complain and be envious, but we would like to state there are on the sugar plantations . . . a large number of laborers who are suffering under a wage of 77 cents a day."

The Honolulu newspapers denounced "Japanese agitators" for calling the strike and made opposition to the strike a test of patriotism. The planters stood firm, evicting about 12,000 people. Then an influenza epidemic spread among the strikers who had found temporary shelter in Honolulu. It is estimated that about 1,200 strikers and their families fell ill. A Filipino labor leader ordered his members back to work, and gradually this strike too

Pearl Harbor was just a Navy coaling station at first

petered out. As a result of the 1920 strike, the plantations made improvements in housing and sanitation conditions and stepped up a welfare program of medical, school, and recreation facilities. In 1924 the Filipinos struck, but this time the Japanese did not support them. The strike turned out to be the bloodiest in Hawaii's history: sixteen strikers and four policemen were killed.

For almost twenty years thereafter there was little labor disturbance or organization on the plantations. A CIO union did win a contract for some workers on one plantation on Kauai in 1940. But the plantations were still largely unorganized when World War II came. As late as 1939, James H. Shoemaker, now a Bank of Hawaii executive, wrote in a United States Labor Department report that the labor attitude of the sugar industry "may best be described as benevolently paternalistic rather than liberal. The history of management in Hawaii, broadly speaking, is one of antagonism to labor organization."

Perhaps never before did the position of the Big Five seem more secure than on the eve of World War II. Their position in the political life of the islands was virtually unchallenged. Shoemaker wrote that "the wealth of the islands is largely in the hands of Caucasians, or, to be more specific, Anglo-Saxons." He pointed to family relationships and interlocking directorates making for a centralization of control which "is not confined to the sugar industry alone, but extends into practically every aspect of the economic life."

And yet beneath the surface unsettling forces were at work. Mainland businesses were beginning to invade Hawaii. There are stories, still making the rounds in Hawaii, that one big national retail chain, unable to buy land for a branch, had to find an innocuous little old lady to act as a front to make the purchase. But the fact is that the chain stores like Sears and Kress were breaking into the Hawaiian market and ending the monopoly of Big Five stores.

Moreover, union organization was growing, especially on the water front and in miscellaneous crafts. There was restlessness among the younger generation of Hawaii's predominantly Oriental population. As *Fortune* put it: "There is an educated generation that is dissatisfied with farm labor yet unable to find white collar work."

There was increasing friction between the men who dominated sugar and the men responsible for making Hawaii a fort. In the old days, when a Navy coaling station was established at Pearl Harbor in 1898, and for some years afterwards, there had been cordial relations between many of the socially prominent families and the higher Navy officers. But now the Army and Navy were expanding all over the place. Pearl Harbor was being rapidly built up. Navy payrolls reached what was for Hawaii the stupendous total of $20,000,000 a year. The Army was spending $25,000,000 a year, and 25,000 troops were stationed at Schofield Barracks. All this was upsetting established economic patterns. The military wanted diversification of crops so that Hawaii could be more self-sustaining in time of war – less sugar and pineapple and more vegetables and other foods. High Navy and Army officers were even advancing a plan to establish a commission form of government over Hawaii with strong military representation.

Fortune concluded its survey of Hawaii by suggesting that if war came the islands would never again be the same. "M-Day would obviously spell disaster for the Big Five," it said. If this prediction turned out to be a bit extreme it was nevertheless perceptive. The old Hawaii was on the verge of drastic changes just as it seemed most firmly fixed in its old ways.

5. *The Great Upheaval*

A bright, popular Japanese boy named Paul had a little trouble with a few of his eighth-grade classmates toward the end of World War II. The final campaign against Japan was in full swing, and anti-Japanese feeling was running high. So some of the boys started calling him "Jap."

The principal of the school talked the problem over with Paul's father and devised a simple strategy. The father happened to have been one of Hawaii's 9,500 AJA's (Americans of Japanese ancestry) who volunteered for service at the outset of the war. He was a wounded veteran of the famed 442nd Regimental Combat Team composed of AJA volunteers from Hawaii and the mainland.

So one morning the father showed up at the school, dressed in a uniform resplendent with medals and campaign ribbons. The principal casually introduced the much-decorated officer as "Paul's father." The kids in Paul's classroom were fascinated, asked questions about the battles his father had fought in, the campaign ribbons, the Purple Heart, the medals. They never called Paul a "Jap" again.

In a small way, the incident illustrates one of the main results of World War II in Hawaii. There had been many doubts about the patriotism of the Japanese, and some nasty rumors. There

Burning and damaged ships at Pearl Harbor on December 7, 1941

were no more questions or rumors after the war. The Japanese now claimed and got the equality they had won in battle.

Hawaii was shaken up by the war as no other part of the United States. It was, after all, our one important territory which withstood enemy attack and knew the meaning of war first hand. Out of the war came not only a heightened unity of all the races and peoples of Hawaii but a greater measure of democracy in every sense.

The plantation workers, long the submerged section of Hawaii's population, organized into unions. They achieved not only substantially higher wages. They also won an enhanced status and for the first time a feeling of participation in the political and social life of the islands. Hawaii's seemingly fixed economic pattern began to change. New industries began to develop, new opportunity began to emerge both for long-time island residents and for mainland newcomers and investors. The conditions for change had long been maturing. It took the war to bring them to the surface. Out of the war emerged the democratic, vital Hawaii of today.

A two-man Japanese submarine washed ashore at Kaneohe Bay on Oahu

Prior to Pearl Harbor, the Japanese were still regarded with suspicion if not hostility by some elements in the local population. There were occasional slurs in the newspapers on the Americanism of the Oriental population, and some high-ranking military officials made no secret of their belief that Hawaii's Japanese were the Achilles heel of our Pacific defenses. In a blistering statement in 1932, Rear Admiral Yates Stirling, Jr., Commander of United States Naval Forces in Hawaii, referred to "the acute threat of sabotage or of anti-American actions by hostile elements of the local population." He added that "years of study by civilian, military and naval authorities of the probable attitude of certain of the island-born Orientals has led to the conclusion that but doubtful reliance can be placed on their loyalty to the United States in the event of war with an Oriental power."

Fortunately, such attitudes were not general among either the military or the civilian population. There were no plans for mass roundups of Japanese, and there was no hysteria of the type which swept our West Coast when Japanese Americans were indiscriminately shipped off to war relocation camps. Out of a

The wreckage of the USS *Arizona* after the attack

population of 160,000 Japanese in Hawaii, only 1,441 were picked up for internment during the entire war. There were acts of prejudice and reprisals, of course. There was some pressure against wearing kimonos and using the Japanese language. The Japanese-language schools attended by thousands of island children were shut down for the duration. The Japanese-language press was suspended briefly, then permitted to publish under close supervision. A number of Japanese political figures felt it expedient to withdraw from public life.

There were, to be sure, a few instances of disloyalty; and there were some wild rumors that Japanese aviators shot down near Honolulu in December 1941 were wearing the class rings of local schools and that arrows had been cut in the cane fields by Japanese plantation workers to guide enemy planes straight to Pearl Harbor. According to Robert L. Shivers, special agent in charge of the Federal Bureau of Investigation in Hawaii during

The crew of the attack aircraft carrier *Bennington* stands at attention in salute to the 1,102 men entombed in the *Arizona* on December 7

the war, "there was not an iota of truth" in any of these rumors. "There was not one single act of sabotage committed against the war effort in the Hawaiian Islands during the course of the entire war," he said. "Nor was there any fifth column activity in existence or in evidence here."

Out of the first thirty-six civilians killed by bombs and shrapnel falling on Honolulu, twenty were Japanese. But it soon became apparent that the Japanese-American response to the Japanese attack on Pearl Harbor was precisely the same as that of all other Americans on the islands – only more so. Among the first heroes of the attack were two AJA Navy Yard workers at Pearl Harbor, later cited for bravery, who helped man a machine gun, feeding ammunition tirelessly though their hands were badly burned.

The entire population of Hawaii rallied to the war effort. There was some grumbling at the severe restrictions imposed by martial law, but only because it was felt that they were both unnecessary and unconstitutional. Civilian defense was a more serious thing here than on mainland United States. Red Cross and war bond drives had a more immediate meaning. Victory Gardens were more widespread. Everybody did something for the war effort, including the older noncombatant Japanese.

Admiral Stirling had complained that the presence of Buddhist temples in Hawaii was a sign that the Japanese "consider themselves primarily subordinate to the country of their racial origin." But now old Japanese men and women came to Buddhist temples — to leave offerings and pray for American victory. It was traditional among the Japanese to give tea to friends and relatives on the forty-ninth day after the death of a member of the family. Now the parents of Sergeant Joseph Takata, killed in action in North Africa, gave $400 to the Red Cross instead. That was a big sum for plantation workers, and soon other island Japanese were following suit.

At first the young AJA's were kept out of the armed forces. Students at the University of Hawaii and the four Honolulu high schools were displeased when the Hawaii Territorial Guard was dissolved — partly because of criticism that these sons of enemy aliens were being permitted to guard critically important defense installations. So these AJA's wrote to General Delos C. Emmons, commanding officer of the Army in Hawaii, that they were "deeply disappointed" and added: "We know but one loyalty and that is to the Stars and Stripes. We wish to do our part as loyal Americans in every way possible." General Emmons accepted the offer. The group formed the Varsity Victory Volunteers and was assigned some of the dirtiest work with a regiment of engineers as railroad-track layers and common laborers. When AJA's were accepted into the armed forces, most of these youngsters promptly volunteered.

Some 1,300 AJA's were trained in Wisconsin as the 100th Infantry Battalion. In 1943 they were at the Salerno beachhead and fought their way through Italy. Now known as the "Purple Heart Battalion," they were incorporated into the 442nd Regimental Combat Team, made up of AJA volunteers from Hawaii and the

The ILWU Organizing Committee in 1944, planning to send teams of "missionaries" to the outer islands

mainland. Within thirty days, 9,507 AJA's answered a War Department call for 1,500 men for this unit. The Army had to increase the number to 2,600, and even so this was a hand-picked group which included the cream of Hawaii's Japanese, the professionals, the businessmen, the teachers. The 442nd was one of the most highly educated units in the Army, and it was also described by the military officials as "probably the most decorated unit in United States military history." This was the group that fought at Anzio, launched the first infantry attack near the abbey at Monte Cassino early in 1944, and that took San Michele in a night attack. A front-line correspondent of *The New York Times* sent this dispatch from Italy:

> "Latest periodicals reaching the troops quote those who have never heard, shot, or fired at anything bigger than a duck to the effect that all Japanese citizens of the United States should be barred and that 'the only good Jap is a dead one.' This Japanese-American battalion is the best answer to that type of doctrine. These men have not only been fighting with tremendous bravery and bearing all the sufferings and dangers their fellow G.I. soldiers have, but they are serving in a sort of crusade – to make the rest of America understand that they, too, are good and loyal Americans."

There is no doubt that Hawaii's Japanese fought with special daring and courage, and the statistics showed it. According to the final count of Hawaii's war casualties, 80 percent of those killed and 88 percent of those wounded were AJA's. The AJA's, including those from the mainland, received 1,580 decorations, apart from 4,500 or more Purple Hearts.

After the war these young Japanese began to play a prominent role in Hawaii's professional and political life, and you meet them today in the legislature and in business circles. One of them, Daniel K. Inouye, has recently won election to the Congress of the United States.

As a result of the war, Hawaii's peoples became one. FBI Agent Shivers put it this way in summing up his war-time observations:

> "Hawaii's people of various racial ancestries can and do work together, particularly in the face of a major crisis.
>
> "What goes on in the countries of their ancestors is of minor consequence to them as compared to what goes on in their own country, the United States of America. The latter is their major concern as Americans."

Early in 1944 small groups of men from Honolulu began to invade the neighboring islands. They were Hawaiians, Japanese, Filipinos, Caucasians — union longshoremen from Honolulu, members of Harry Bridges' International Longshoremen's & Warehousemen's Union (ILWU) which had organized the Honolulu docks during the 1930's and was now firmly entrenched. They were armed only with small white cards, stating, "This Is the Law," and citing the provisions of the Wagner Labor Relations Act about the right of workers to join unions. Perhaps a little ironically, these organizers said they were doing "missionary work."

The plantation workers had been waiting for union organization a long time. In some respects, martial law had aggravated old grievances. Shortly after Pearl Harbor, the military governor froze all wages, and imposed fines and prison terms on all who left their jobs without formal release. As soon as civil government began to return, the ILWU organizers seized their opportunity —

and the field and mill hands flocked into the union. In National Labor Relations Board elections, sugar workers voted for the union by better than twenty-five to one.

It was no wonder. The union claimed that before organization field hands on some sugar plantations were getting as little as 25 cents an hour, that wages of skilled mechanics were as low as 50 cents an hour. The first industry-wide contract in 1945 established a base rate of 43½ cents an hour for unskilled workers, 41 cents on the island of Hawaii. From the sugar plantations the ILWU went into the pineapple industry, organizing first the canneries and then the field workers, winning an industry-wide contract in 1946.

Before long the ILWU became Hawaii's biggest labor organization — as well as its most controversial. The three industries under its jurisdiction are sugar, pineapple, and longshore. It claims about 24,000 members as against 3,500 for the International Brotherhood of Teamsters and approximately 15,000 for all AFL-CIO unions. The construction boom of the past few years has led to a rapid growth of AFL-CIO building trades unions. As a result, the AFL-CIO has begun to challenge the dominant position of the ILWU in island labor affairs.

Less than fifteen years after the rise of the ILWU, the Hawaiian Sugar Planters' Association reported: "The Islands' sugar workers are the highest paid sugar workers in the world. And this is on a year-round basis." Field workers in Hawaii average $17 a day including pension, medical, and other fringe benefits. This is twice the average for field workers in Florida, almost three times as much as in Louisiana, and about four times as much as in Puerto Rico.

But more than wages was involved in the union's spectacular growth after World War II. The old spirit of paternalism was now outdated. The system of perquisites was abolished after some hard bargaining on the cash value of the services offered the workers. The workers preferred to get their wages in cash and pay their rent in company houses or buy their own. What rankled them was their lack of independence, their treatment as inferiors, the complete domination on the part of the plantation

Leaders of Teamsters Local 996 – Art Rutledge, head of the Teamsters in Hawaii, is seated in center

management, the abuses of the lunas or supervisors.

A Filipino union organizer told me he had been a supervisory worker for nineteen years. "One day," he said, "I was called into the main office and told there was a big cut in the work force and that I would now have to be a canecutter. I joined the union right away. The superintendent asked, 'How could you join the union? Where is your loyalty to the plantation?' After what they did to me, I told him, 'I am a field worker now, and I will join with the other field workers.' "

Another worker explains, "I don't agree that guys join the union just because they see the dollar. Guys find the union a way of expressing themselves and their ideas. Where before a guy had to shut up or get out, now guys get the union if they need any help in settling grievances."

The union gave the workers increased status, and made them a part of their communities. Union organizers in Hilo on the Big Island or in Wailuku on Maui reminded me somewhat of small-town political leaders on the mainland. They know everybody, stop to chat with every second person on the street, take pride in the community. Tom Yagi, the union organizer on Maui who helped show me around the island, took me first to the community hospital of which he is chairman, only later to his union headquarters.

While the ILWU has never been as all-powerful politically as is sometimes claimed by critics, it has been influential. Starting in 1944, it has elected some of its members to the legislature and has been successful in working for the passage of social legislation protecting its members. Hawaii is now far ahead of the mainland states in the extension of all social legislation, such as wages and hours, unemployment compensation, and the like, to agricultural workers. ILWU participation in politics has resulted in tangible benefits for its members; it has also given them a sense of power, of direct participation in politics and government.

Oriental workers felt that the union ended old discriminations against them. As a Japanese worker put it, "The union is a good thing because it has opened up opportunities for the Japanese. Before the union came in, few Japanese were able to become lunas. Now the pressure from the union has made for more promotions. Yes, there are bad things about the union, but now at least we can talk and act without fear and be heard." For the Filipinos the union was even more important in opening the doors to advancement.

A major source of the ILWU's strength has been its ability to hold Japanese and Filipinos, Chinese, Portuguese, Puerto Ricans, Hawaiians, and Haoles together in one organization. This had never been done before. National labor organizations had been reluctant to organize Oriental workers, and especially Oriental agricultural workers. Japanese carpenters in Honolulu have charged only recently that their national union is trying to push them around. Whatever else may be said about the ILWU chiefs, they never tolerated discrimination and they insisted on representation of all Hawaii's national and racial groups in union leadership.

One of Hawaii's leading bankers told me, "The islands were over-ripe for union organization. It is our tragedy that it had to be Harry Bridges who got here first."

ILWU leaders discussing contract demands during the 1948 negotiations. Harry Bridges is seated at the table, third from the left; Jack Hall is second from the right

There is a certain irony in the fact that it was Harry Bridges' ILWU, the most militant of labor unions headed by the most radical of labor leaders, which organized most successfully in Hawaii, the most conservative and stalwart of antiunion strongholds. The planters and HSPA had so often in the past branded all union organization as radical that allegations of Communist domination against the ILWU made scarcely a ripple among the plantation workers.

In fact, Bridges and Louis Goldblatt, the union's two mainland leaders, and Jack Hall, its Hawaii director, probably gained in popularity under attack. The ILWU's expulsion from the CIO in 1949 on charges of Communist control had little impact in Hawaii. Hall even survived, without serious challenge to his leadership, a Smith Act trial and conviction in 1954, later overturned by the Ninth United States Circuit Court of Appeals, for advocacy of overthrow of the government by force and violence. The union also has weathered several major strikes without noticeable loss in strength, a sugar strike in 1946, a pineapple strike the next year, a long and hard-fought longshore strike in 1949, and a pro-

Plantation workers discussing their demands during the 1946 strike

longed sugar strike in 1958, sometimes called "the aloha strike." There was less bitterness in 1958 than in past strikes, with a feeling among union men and leaders alike that perhaps it marked the end of the period of turbulent labor relations in Hawaii.

The storms that raged around the ILWU became a top-ranking political issue in Hawaii and an important impediment to statehood. The violent charges and countercharges around the ILWU, originally developed out of the sharp labor battles in the islands, spread to the political arena.

Newspaper editorials have frequently described ILWU leaders as "Communists" and the union as "Communist-dominated." Senator James O. Eastland of Mississippi has called on the members to "throw off the Bridges-Hall leadership and get back into organized labor." Eastland's Senate Internal Security Committee has even called the union "a threat to the security of the United States."

On the other hand, Hawaii's last territorial delegate to Congress, John A. Burns, said that the ILWU "laid the foundations for democracy in the Hawaiian islands" when it organized the

Sugar strikers in 1958 were prepared with lots of rice for their soup kitchens

plantation workers because it "enabled them to realize that they had dignity, they were citizens who had a right to their own activities and the right to participate in such little government as we have. They created the climate that enabled others and themselves to develop the free society that they have."

ILWU spokesmen have maintained consistently that the Communist issue has been "a smoke-screen" for opposition first to union organization and later to statehood. One ILWU leader told me, "I doubt if there are a dozen Communist Party members in Hawaii. The ILWU isn't dominated by any political, social, religious or any other outside force, and Eastland and others who have attacked our union know it."

Alexander G. Budge, president of Castle & Cooke, has said, "I don't know that the actions actually of the union or its leadership are any different from the actions and leadership of other unions as you read of them on the mainland."

While there is controversy about the ILWU leadership, there is very little dispute about the reasons for the union's growth or for the loyalty of the members to their leaders. A pamphlet published by the Hawaii Statehood Commission in 1957 and sharply critical of ILWU leaders put the question of "why a group of 24,000 Americans of proven loyalty have countenanced the leadership of Harry Bridges and Jack Hall." The pamphlet continued, "The answer the workers give is that ILWU members and their families have enjoyed undisputed economic gains under this stewardship, accompanied by better working conditions and improved living conditions."

In any case, there seems little doubt that the ILWU is a major force in Hawaii – one of the forces which after World War II helped shake up the old patriarchal order and break down the caste and racial lines that had divided its peoples.

The war brought other changes, equally decisive in their impact on the old Hawaii – particularly the influx of new people and new capital. War workers and servicemen came by the hundreds of thousands; many of them stayed or returned later to settle down. The newcomers had little respect for the established Haole families, the Kamaainas. Old names no longer carried as much weight in politics or in social life.

The influx of capital had begun before the war. The chain stores had started coming in, and the United States Maritime Commission had attacked Matson's virtual monopoly on steamship freight and passenger business with the islands. The federal government took over the old Dollar Line, and reorganized it as the privately owned American President Lines, which has now emerged as a competitor to Matson. Now the airlines have come to the fore as the major passenger carrier to Hawaii.

The war accelerated the development of new companies engaged in the handling of defense cargoes and in military construction. The military establishment continued after the war to remain Hawaii's biggest industry, replacing sugar and pineapple in first place. Both military and civilian construction became major factors in the economy. Tourism started to boom after the war. The whole economy experienced far-reaching changes.

Faced with growing competition, the Big Five firms brought in new managers from the mainland. Chinese and Japanese busi-

Matson passenger liners face increasing competition after the war

ness firms developed in insurance, banking, real estate, construction, and other lines. It would be an exaggeration to say that sugar and pineapple were no longer extremely important to Hawaii's economy, or that the Big Five no longer played a major role. But the old interests were no longer as dominant, and certainly they had no monopoly in either the economic or political life of Hawaii.

With the influx of outside capital, the new role of organized labor, and the increased status of Hawaii's Oriental peoples, new forces came into play in Hawaii. The Big Five could properly claim credit for having helped to build up Hawaii. But in the new growth following World War II, old types of control were challenged and the new democratic Hawaii emerged.

6. Boom in Paradise

It was a rather unusual debate that took place in the Waianae High School near Honolulu on that warm May evening in 1959. Facing each other were two of the titans of Hawaiian business — and they were vying for the support of a crowd of small farmers, fishermen, and miscellaneous workers of a rather run-down former plantation area.

The two antagonists were Walter F. Dillingham, patriarch of the formidable Dillingham clan, immaculately groomed, still stiff-necked, sharp-spoken, and clear-minded at 84, and a 77-year-old youngster named Henry J. Kaiser, a big, boisterous, somewhat rumpled newcomer to the economic wars in Hawaii.

Kaiser and the Dillinghams were fighting what has since become known as the battle of the cement plants. Since before World War II, Dillingham's giant Hawaiian Dredging & Construction Company had been buying Kaiser cement from the Permanente Cement Company. Kaiser had established a virtual monopoly on cement for Hawaii's booming construction industry by bringing in his product on his own bottoms from California. But now Dillingham was threatening to take away Kaiser's cement business, and Kaiser in turn was threatening to invade Dillingham's heavy construction business.

Early in 1959 Dillingham teamed up with other Hawaiian and

mainland interests to announce construction of a new $12,000,000 cement plant on Oahu. Then Kaiser announced only a few days afterwards that he, too, would build a $12,000,000 cement plant. The only hitch was that rezoning would be required in the Waianae district where Kaiser proposed to locate, and Dillingham threw his considerable influence into the scales against a rezoning permit.

So Kaiser decided to take his case directly to the community, and Walter Dillingham drove out to Waianae with his son, Ben, to answer this interloper in person. It was just a few days after Ben had told me that Hawaii still has new economic frontiers; and that debate in the high school certainly seemed to prove it.

Kaiser told the community meeting that he planned not only to put up the cement plant but also to build one of his modern medical clinics in the area. "I wonder," he said, "whether Mr. Ben Dillingham and his associates have the influence to override the overwhelming desire expressed by the people of this area to locate the new industry here."

Walter Dillingham, every inch the wealthy kamaaina born and bred in Hawaii, snapped into the microphone in his hand, "I don't think it's a very nice thing for a visitor to Hawaii, no matter how many millions he's spent here, to attack a son of mine and of Hawaii."

The issue was put to a vote, and the meeting went on record overwhelmingly in favor of the Kaiser plant. It meant jobs for the local population, mainly Oriental and part-Hawaiian. The clinic was a big consideration with the crowd. As one man put it, "We are a working-class people in this area. We haven't had proper medical care here. Every time one of our wives or daughters gets pregnant, it's a 50-50 chance the baby will be born in a car on the way to a Honolulu hospital."

It is something new for Hawaii to have this kind of public debate. It is also something new for Hawaii, which in the past has always imported almost all manufactured goods, to face the prospect of getting not one but two big cement plants. This is symptomatic of the spectacular economic growth in Hawaii since World War II. There are many new and unforeseen business

Business and government buildings in Honolulu's financial center

opportunities. But there are also new entrepreneurs, like Henry Kaiser, to take advantage of them – in sharp competition with the Big Five and the Dillinghams.

Kaiser is not too well liked by some of the old-timers in Hawaii. They consider him arrogant and overaggressive. But he enjoys a considerable popularity with the man on the street, and many of the Oriental businessmen welcome him as an ally against the older, entrenched interests.

One of the current legends around Honolulu is that Kaiser became interested in our newest state after his second marriage when he came to Hawaii with his bride for a belated honeymoon and couldn't find suitably sumptuous accommodations. The suite he wanted at the Royal Hawaiian Hotel was taken. He is supposed to have considered buying the hotel outright. But after settling down in humbler quarters, he compromised on building the biggest hotel in Honolulu – the Hawaiian Village – with part of the big new tourist complex finished within ninety days.

Kaiser has spent $14,000,000 on the Hawaiian Village so far — and his plans call for a total of $100,000,000 on new hotel facilities. He filled in land to make room for his hotel, and he proposed to create some 200 acres more the same way. His Kaiser Foundation Hospital, not far from the hotel, has extended to Honolulu the low-cost prepaid medical plan he introduced on the mainland West Coast. While devising new schemes and enterprises, he is building a palatial estate at Maunalua Bay on Oahu. His most ambitious project to date is Hawaii-Kai, "a $350,000,000 resort city for 50,000 people" in the Koko Head and Maunalua sections of Oahu.

From his suite atop the Hawaiian Village he issues statements full of capital letters, exclamation points, and enthusiasm:

> "Envision the new and greater State of Hawaii that is being built! Tremendous jobs of construction lie immediately ahead.
>
> "Think of the resort hotels and new buildings to house every kind of business and profession that must be constructed throughout the islands to meet the demands of Hawaii's Vacation Industry alone. . . .
>
> "This historic year of Statehood ushers in Hawaii's Time of Destiny!"

Kaiser's statements reflect something more than his own buoyant personality. It is symptomatic of the boom spirit in Hawaii, of new industries, new capital, new construction. The boom has continued without interruption during the 1950's. A report by James H. Shoemaker, vice-president and economic expert of the Bank of Hawaii, tells the story of a decade of growth: personal income has increased 66 percent, bank deposits by 70 percent, tourist trade by 238 percent, construction by 102 percent, manufacturing by 60 percent, civilian population by 22 percent. Moreover, the Bank of Hawaii's business research department forecasts an over-all growth of 40 percent in the island's economy between 1959 and 1970.

Some of the Big Five interests were apparently caught napping by the big postwar upsurge in Hawaii, especially by the expansion of the past decade. This is not true of the Dillinghams.

Hawaii's sugar scientists have developed numerous new machines. This one digs a furrow, plants seed cane, and gives it a squirt of fertilizer to start it on its way

They are deeply involved in some of the biggest and most imaginative of the new projects – such as the 50-acre, $28,000,000 Ala Moana shopping center which will have more shopping facilities than the whole downtown Honolulu area combined and which reflects the population trend away from the center of town.

You can easily get into an argument over the extent to which the Big Five interests are participating in the boom and remain dominant in the economy.

"Don't let them kid you," one government official from the mainland, who has had some unpleasant rows with representatives of the older economic interests, told me. "The Big Five still run this place."

At the opposite extreme was a Chinese business leader who said, "The Big Five are played out. Their blood has run thin. They're incompetent. They've had to import mainland capital and mainland personnel. I meet with them on various committees all the time, and, believe me, they don't have what it takes any more. It takes them hours to arrive at decisions which should take five minutes."

Sugar planters have invested heavily in irrigation

The most objective business opinion seems to be that the Big Five have been seriously weakened but still remain a significant factor in the new economy of Hawaii. Thus, *Business Week* points out that "the Big Five still own or control 25 out of the 29 sugar plantations, five of the eight pineapple canneries and the Matson Navigation Company, which dominates shipping to and from the mainland." They are also important in banking, the retail trade, real estate, and especially in ownership and control of land.

Sugar and pineapple, it should be remembered, are still the most decisive and stable industries in the islands. Sugar production is estimated at $150,000,000 a year, and pineapple at $125,-000,000. These are substantial chunks of an economy functioning at about $1,500,000,000 a year. Moreover, they are healthy and prosperous industries which have adapted themselves well to the higher labor costs resulting from mechanization, with about a

Special trucks bring bulk sugar from mills to a storage plant where it is unloaded mechanically

third as many workers producing the same amount of sugar as before the war. There is nothing sleepy or backward about Hawaii's large-scale agriculture. It can meet competition anywhere in the world.

It is in the newer industries which have been coming up in recent years that the Big Five interests play a lesser role. Mainland capital has been pouring in at an ever-increasing rate, about $200,000,000 in the last few years alone. Local Japanese and Chinese business interests, often in combination with mainland investors, are also playing a more prominent role in the current expansion.

Matson's monopoly of the maritime tourist traffic to Hawaii has been undermined by the big airlines such as Pan American,

Honolulu Harbor

United, and Northwest, which now take most of the passengers to and from Hawaii. The Sheraton hotel chain has bought Matson's four Waikiki hotels, including the Royal Hawaiian.

Mainland firms, as well as the Dillinghams and other local concerns, have shared in the construction boom spurred by military installations, new hotels, new commercial buildings, and new residential housing. The construction industry is now one of the biggest in Hawaii. It has almost tripled in the past decade, rising from less than $70,000,000 in 1950 to about $200,000,000 in 1959. Military construction has, of course, been an important factor in this boom. Now nearing completion is a $100,000,000 housing program for military personnel and their families.

Defense expenditures have outpaced the sugar, pineapple, or any other industry. The military establishment is now in a sense Hawaii's biggest industry. In 1959 alone it poured $327,000,000 into the islands' economy, accounting for well over a fifth of all business activity. Hawaii is now the center for all American military forces in the Far East. Army, Navy, and Air Force operations have their headquarters in Hawaii under

Sampans owned by local fishermen anchored at Kewalo basin, Honolulu. Commercial fishing may develop into one of Hawaii's more important industries

Admiral Harry D. Felt, commander in chief of the Pacific. About 50,000 members of the armed forces are stationed in Hawaii, and the armed forces provide civilian employment to about 20,000 more.

Almost as important as the military in stimulating business was the postwar boom in tourism – or what people in Hawaii like to call the visitor industry. Tourism had for many years been a modest but relatively unimportant addition to Hawaii's basic plantation economy. In 1922 there were some 10,000 visitors to Hawaii, the record figure up to that time. Encouraged by the Hawaii Tourist Bureau, later the Hawaii Visitors Bureau, tourism gradually increased. During the 1929-33 depression, however, it dropped off disastrously, picked up again, then was cut off by World War II. But since the war the rise in the number of visitors has been sensational, starting with 15,000 in 1946 and going up every year up to a high point in 1959 of more than 200,000 visitors spending more than $100,000,000.

Sales of muumuus and aloha shirts are sparking a growing garment industry

The tourists and the military together have made necessary the expansion of all kinds of service trades and industries. This has created more jobs and has made it possible, as the economists put it, for Hawaii to balance its trade with the mainland. One of Hawaii's long-standing ailments as an island economy is that it tends to import more than it exports. But in recent years, the item of "invisible" exports – the services provided to the armed forces and to travelers – has increased the wealth coming into Hawaii.

New industries have been coming in. Standard Oil is building a $40,000,000-a-year refinery which may serve the entire Pacific area, saving transportation costs of shipping oil from Sumatra to the West Coast and then back to Hawaii and other Pacific areas. A new steel rolling mill is going up on Oahu, and an electric furnace is in prospect. New electronic plants are in operation, or are in prospect. A $15,000,000-a-year garment industry, exploiting the vogue for aloha shirts and muumuus, has developed.

Pandanus leaves are being dried, prior to being made into gift items by local craftsmen. Sales of local handicrafts to tourists have been booming

While transportation and raw-material problems will undoubtedly keep Hawaii from developing any major heavy industry, economic planners believe there is plenty of room for a light fabricating industry. In fact, high freight rates make it cheaper to send in the raw materials to fabricate and assemble certain steel products, electronic devices, and household items in Hawaii than to waste valuable cargo space in shipping in the finished products.

This is one of the prospects that Hawaii's businessmen and economists bank on to continue the islands' present prosperity. There is optimism about the future – but also some nervousness based in part on the experience of the past. The fact is that the boom followed a serious postwar depression, one that was considerably worse than the 1949-50 economic decline on the mainland. War spending, reaching a peak of $800,000,000 during 1944, sent Hawaii's economy zooming upwards. But when defense expenditures were slashed to $224,000,000 in 1946 and reached a low of $148,000,000 in 1950, the result was a real crisis in Hawaii's economy.

One of the largest industrial cranes in the world in operation at the Pearl Harbor Navy Yard

Cuts in military spending coincided with drastic reductions in the plantation labor force due to mechanization. Introduction of new machinery for weeding, harvesting, and processing raw sugar reduced sugar industry employment from a prewar peak of more than 50,000 to about 17,000 at present. Pineapple mechanization was not so drastic, but there was also a reduction in that industry's work force. The long 1949 water-front strike added to the dismal picture. More than a sixth of Hawaii's labor force was unemployed in 1950.

Military spending triggered recovery and boom. But memories of depression lingered on. Business economists like Shoemaker and government planners began at that point to issue the numerous reports and surveys which have now become one of Hawaii's minor industries. The volume of printed material suggests that the new state is quite sophisticated when it comes to promotion and public relations; much of this material is designed to interest new business and investment. But it also suggests a

One of Pearl Harbor's landmarks is the submarine base escape training tank, housing a 100-foot column of water

certain amount of nervousness about the stability of Hawaii's current boom and a conviction of the need for economic expansion and diversification.

It is generally conceded that certain aspects of the boom will taper off. The present pace of new construction is expected to slow up within a couple of years. For example, the $100,000,000 military housing program is nearing completion. Downtown business construction may also be past its peak. On the other hand, hotel and home construction will probably continue for quite a while.

One of the big intangibles is what will happen to defense spending, which accounts for more than a fifth of all business activity in Hawaii. When you include more than $75,000,000 in nonmilitary federal expenditures in Hawaii and another $150,000,000 for the functions of state and local governments, you get about a third of Hawaii's $1,500,000,000 economy directly dependent on the government. Governor William F. Quinn told me frankly he was quite worried about a continuation of this proportion as a long-range proposition.

Shoemaker and other experts do not foresee any sudden contraction in the military establishment. Military spokesmen also believe that Hawaii will maintain its importance as United States command headquarters in the Far East as a logistic center for repairs and supplies and as a major training base. They told me that radar, missile, and other technological advances will almost certainly result in construction of new facilities without in their opinion reducing the number of men stationed in the islands.

On the other hand, in the present state of world affairs military spending continues to have its imponderables. When I started inquiring about this problem, I was met with knowing smiles and vague assurances that there were interesting developments in the offing. The story broke a few days later that the Army was planning eight new Nike bases on Oahu. But then the Senate Armed Services Committee turned thumbs down on fifty new Nike bases throughout the United States, including the eight on Oahu. The committee wanted the Defense Department to make a choice between the Army's Nike missiles and the Air Force Bomarc. Finally, the bases were reinstated. But the element of uncertainty in the defense program remains.

The natural limits on Hawaii's economic potential also trouble her planners. As is often pointed out, Hawaii has plenty of scenery, good soil, and good climate – but not much else. There is no oil, and there are few mineral resources. Bauxite and titanium have been discovered, and there may be industrial possibilities for lava rock and ash. But on the whole Hawaii lacks the raw materials for extensive manufacturing. Its supply of water is also inadequate and uneven. As an island community it is further limited. Its own home market is relatively small, and transportation costs make it difficult to develop an extensive industry for export.

Perhaps most important, Hawaii is not a very big place to begin with, and quite a bit of it, especially on the Big Island, is volcanic wasteland or semidesert. Much of the land is owned by

Aerial view of the Pearl Harbor naval shipyard looking toward Hickam Air Force Base

the military, the federal government, and the state. And a good deal of it is held by large estates, like the Bishop Estate or the Campbell Estate, which are a holdover of the old feudal days in Hawaii. Most of these lands were the property of the crown or the nobility or became so after the division of land under the Great Mahele; later they passed into the hands of the old Haole families. The magnitude of these holdings may be imagined when it is recalled that the Bishop Estate alone has about 350,000 acres — almost ten percent of Hawaii's total of 4,100,000 acres and more than the total of land under cultivation on the islands.

As a result of this concentration of ownership, it is extremely difficult to get hold of land for agriculture, industry, or real estate development. Control of land by the old families is a continuing source of irritation in Hawaii. The charge is often made that the estates don't use the land—and either refuse to sell it or to do so at exorbitant prices. As *Business Week* points out, "Real Estate in Hawaii is assessed according to current use of the land rather than actual market value as reflected in sales. Thus, the owners can afford to keep tracts off the market and can maintain rentals by rationing their leases like diamonds." A legislative committee on land reform has charged that large landholders follow the "dubious practice of defining the 'fair market value' of their property at a very low figure for tax purposes and at a high figure for condemnation purposes." It cites the case of a piece of land owned by the Campbell Estate which was valued at $25,000 but was sold for more than $1,000,000 to Standard Oil as the site for a new refinery.

Feuds about land are an everyday occurrence in Hawaii. The Waikiki hotel interests are in constant battle with the Army, which holds tenaciously to a choice parcel of Waikiki Beach acreage at Fort De Russy. The land is used as a recreation center for soldiers. "Bad public relations," says a Navy officer off the record. But the Army retorts that servicemen are entitled to recreation facilities on the beach just as much as tourists.

In any case, land is at a premium, and sells as high as $3 to $3.50 a square foot in Honolulu, up to $40 a square foot on Waikiki Beach. Even at that price it is not always available. Many people lease the land on which their homes are built—and even the sugar plantations lease about 40 percent of the land they use.

Advocates of land reform believe that this situation can be eased, that legislation enacted by the legislature at its 1949 session will make more land available for homes through condemnation proceedings or purchase by the state government. Some businessmen also believe that the impact of an elected state government on the judiciary will make for rulings which in the long run will tend to break up some of the larger estates.

What makes the scramble for land somewhat ironical is that there is land available for economic expansion—but not on Oahu. It is on the outer islands. The Big Island of Hawaii alone is almost twice as large as all the other islands put together. But the business boom of recent years has been wholly confined to Oahu. It has not spread to the other islands. Developing their economy is part of the over-all goal of the planners. They see prospects for light industry, truck farming, and more tourism on the neighbor islands.

As Hawaii became a state, there was virtually no unemployment on its lush islands, and it had a per capita income of $1,876 a year, higher than 26 states. The signs of prosperity are evident in new homes, new cars, new television sets, in the individual well being of Hawaii's peoples both in Honolulu and on the plantations. Maintaining this prosperity without some of the sharp ups and downs of the past is one of the principal concerns of its new state government.

Generally, the planners aim at a balanced economic development which will keep the boom going. They believe that the number of tourists will keep rising and that the visitor industry will perhaps become Hawaii's biggest. They also hope to see a rise in Hawaii's importance as a technical, cultural, and trade center for the East.

7. The Neglected Isles

When most people talk about Hawaii, they are usually referring to that narrow strip of filled-in land called Waikiki Beach with about one hundredth of one percent of the new state's area. At most they include the city of Honolulu and the island of Oahu on which it is situated — amounting to about one tenth of Hawaii's area.

Rarely do visitors to Hawaii pay much attention to what people on Oahu call the neighbor islands. Yet these islands are important for many reasons. It is here that most of Hawaii's sugar and almost half its pineapple are produced. It is here that much of Hawaii's future lies in terms of unused resources and land. It is also here that the visitor will find the most authentic magic and lure of this island fleet.

In recent years the outer islands have been neglected. As Oahu has flourished, they appear to have become a backwater. More and more of the commercial life of the islands has been concentrated on Oahu. Oahu now has more than 75 percent of the population of the new state, 90 percent of the manufacturing, 92 percent of the construction, 85 percent of the retailing, and almost 92 percent of the tourist business.

The latter fact particularly makes people on the outer islands rather bitter. They feel that they are neglected by tourists from

At a Hawaiian fishing party called a hukulau on Kauai, visitors help islanders pull in the giant net

the mainland. They feel that the Hawaii Visitors Bureau and the travel agencies deliberately slight them and concentrate all their efforts on Oahu – despite the really magnificent attractions the less crowded, less spoiled other islands have to offer. Spokesmen for the Hawaii Visitors Bureau and other groups answer that they do their best for the outer islands but that Oahu as the center of Hawaii's economic life has become the magnet attracting business and tourists.

It is a strange paradox. Oahu, the metropolis of the islands, is booming. But the situation on the neighbor islands is one of mild contraction. Except for an occasional new hotel, there are few signs of construction there. Practically no new plants are being located there. Oahu's population has been growing. The popula-

Public school in a plantation community

tion of Hawaii, Kauai, Maui, Molokai, and Lanai is slowly declining. And most important, it is the young people who are leaving.

I met two Japanese nurses at the community hospital in Maui, intelligent young women in their early twenties. They study music. They like to read. But they are plainly bored in Maui.

"What do you do in the evenings?"
"Well, there isn't too much to do."
"Do you go out much?"
"Well, there are very few young men to go out with here."
"What are your plans for the future?"
"We've been thinking of going to Oahu – or maybe even to the mainland. There isn't much of a future here for advancement or for marriage."

This is typical of what one finds on the outer islands. Young people leave for jobs elsewhere. Parents save to send their children to the university, and are reconciled to the thought that they won't come back. There is little for the young to come back to.

Homes in a plantation community

Oahu has been little affected in recent years by the cutbacks on the plantations due to mechanization. The declining job market in sugar has been more than compensated for by the boom in construction and other industries. But on the other islands mechanization has made a more profound impact.

It isn't that there has been acute suffering or mass unemployment. Agreements reached by the ILWU and the Big Five have eased the effects of mechanization. There has been severance pay for those who were eliminated from industry. Older workers have been able to retire on pensions. A repatriation plan has helped foreign-born workers who wanted to return home, and many did go back to the Philippines; some with substantial cash payments from the plantations.

But plantation jobs are unattractive for the younger people and there have not been many of those. Practically no new op-

Huge cranes pick up sugar cane and dump it into waiting trucks

portunities have been opening up for the young people. The contraction of the labor force on the plantations has led to a general economic stagnation on the outer islands. There are a few hopeful signs, however, on the horizon. A second deep-water port on the Big Island was nearing completion in the summer of 1959. Land values around the city of Hilo were booming. With statehood, renewed attention was being paid to the special plight of all the outer islands.

Far-sighted Hawaiians would like to see a scattering of many of the facilities now concentrated on Oahu. For example, they believe that not all military installations need be clustered around Pearl Harbor or on Oahu, that at least some could be moved to the other islands. They also maintain that recreation facilities for the military could be built outside Oahu. Military spokesmen point to one recreation camp for servicemen beautifully situated in the volcano area on the Big Island, but they assert that servicemen are more drawn to the bright lights of Honolulu.

Now a mechanical pineapple planting machine has been devised

Important possibilities for the economy of the outer islands are offered by bolstering truck farming and fostering Hawaii's specialty crops such as coffee, macadamia nuts, passion fruit, guava, mangoes, and papaya. Diversified agriculture is already one of Hawaii's bigger industries, and runs to close to $50,000,000 a year — with cattle and dairy products accounting for more than two thirds. Coffee runs about $7,000,000; vegetables, fruits, nuts, and rice make up about $8,000,000.

Hawaii's farms, except for a few large ranches like the great Parker cattle ranch on the Big Island, generally run small. With their luxuriant tropical vegetation, they also look quite different from the rolling wheat fields or the neatly terraced farm lands we are accustomed to see in much of the United States.

Makoto Nitahara, a 33-year-old farmer near Hilo on the Big Island, was picked by the Hawaii Junior Chamber of Commerce as Hawaii's young farmer of the year a couple of years ago to go to Des Moines as the guest of the chamber there. He told me

Roundup on the Parker Ranch in the Big Island – second biggest ranch under the American flag

that he was the smallest of the five hundred farmers there from all over the country. On his twenty-eight acres he has 7,000 chickens, bananas, passion fruit, tangerines, even has an acre of anthuriums, the big red flowers with the waxen sheen you see in exclusive mainland florist shops. Nitahara told me he bought his land for $100 an acre in 1949, with the help of a government loan. It was a bargain. Now the land is worth three or four times that.

Nitahara studied scientific agriculture under the GI Bill of Rights. He tries to utilize every inch of ground, and he and his wife work extremely hard. An enterprising fellow, he obtained the beds for his anthuriums and other improvements through a deal with the sugar workers during their 1958 strike. For several weeks he had crews of as many as forty men working all day – in return for truckloads of eggs, bananas, and vegetables to strikers' families. He told me that in 1958 he netted about $12,000 – much of which he put back into equipment and machinery.

While Nitahara's success suggests the possibilities of small-

Sugar planters co-operate to maintain the famed HSPA Experiment Station where new uses are devised for cane products. Here sugar is being grown under controlled conditions

scale farming in Hawaii, it is by no means typical. Coffee ranches are considerably smaller than his twenty-eight acres, as little as four or five acres on the Kona coast of the Big Island. The small coffee ranchers, mainly Japanese, have very bad years and very good ones as prices fluctuate wildly. This is true of most of the growers of Hawaii's specialty crops.

Apparently one of the difficulties is the inability of the small farmers on the Big Island and on the other islands as well to get together to plan production and marketing. I was told about the ups and downs of farmers who raise vanda orchids, in great demand for leis. One year right after World War II they sold the vandas for $1.00 a dozen or more. So all the farmers started growing them. Then the prices came crashing down. The same cycle has been repeated in many other specialty crops.

Hawaii's small farmers on the outer islands lack price supports or subsidies, nor do they have the machinery for sufficient pro-

A fishpond on Kauai Island – said to have been built by the Menehunes, the legendary little people who worked at night

motion and advertising of their specialty crops which could undoubtedly command a good market on the mainland. Hawaii's agriculture still seems to have plenty of room for growth and diversification, but the development of its possibilities may well depend on more effective organization by its farmers plus some form of government aid. While there is some truck farming on Oahu, the future of small farming will on the whole be on the neighbor islands.

The sugar industry has been resourceful in exploring another prospect which could be beneficial to all the islands. This is the industrial use of the waste sugar cane, called bagasse, out of which all the juice has been pounded and squeezed and rolled. There is in operation in Hilo on the Big Island a highly mechanized plant which produces wallboard and acoustical board from bagasse. Owned by the Flintkote Company, this plant competes successfully in terms of price and quality with main-

There are plenty of quiet spots for fishing or meditation on the neighbor islands

land plants operated by the same firm as well as with other mainland manufacturers. Under active investigation at a pilot plant in Washington state is a project for the manufacture of paper from bagasse. Bagasse and molasses have been used for poultry feed, and sugar chemistry may well open new horizons for cane by-products.

But it is in their appeal to tourists and older people from the mainland looking for a place to retire that the outer islands have perhaps their greatest opportunity.

There is a good deal of talk in Hawaii about competing with Florida and Southern California in attracting older folks. One point of dispute concerns whether the appeal should be made mainly to couples in the middle- and upper-income brackets or whether people of modest means should also be invited to come and settle down. Generally speaking, businessmen on the neighbor islands would be delighted to have retired folks with as little as $300 or $400 a month, while the tendency among economic

Driving through the fern forest in the Big Island's volcanic region

planners and business spokesmen on Oahu is to aim at the group with at least double that income.

But there is little argument about the fact that it is the outer islands which offer the best kind of possibilities for this kind of program. Life is less expensive than on Oahu. It is less crowded, more leisurely. The climate is about the same, rivaling anything anywhere in the United States for people seeking to get away from the extremes of cold and heat on most parts of the mainland.

It is on these islands also that many tourists will find the Hawaii of their dreams. It is here for the most part they will find

The venturesome take some horseback trips right on into the Haleakala crater on Maui Island

the quiet, secluded beaches, the tropical scenery, the Hawaii that existed before Waikiki became a cluster of modern skyscraper hotels and Honolulu a modern, bustling city.

While there has been a great build-up of the Polynesian aspect of Hawaii's appeal, there is really nothing of this left at Waikiki and very little on Oahu except in museums. It is on the neighbor islands that one can still get a feeling of the old Hawaii: in villages where Hawaiians raise taro and fish in outrigger canoes and live a life free of some of the modern anxieties and problems. There one can see authentic remnants of the Polynesian past — the City of Refuge on the Kona coast of the Big Island where fugitives were able to find sanctuary, old heiaus and other relics on Kauai and Maui.

It is on the neighbor islands, too, that one finds some of the

The fern grotto on Kauai's Wailua River – a favorite spot for tourists

scenic wonders of Hawaii. On the Big Island one can see the great volcanic mountains of Mauna Loa and Mauna Kea, their crests sometimes covered with snow; and one can drive right up to the gaping Kilauea crater through tropical forests of great fern trees. On Maui there is the spectacular Iao Needle, the great Haleakala crater, and the silversword with its glistening rapier-like leaves. The great Waimea Canyon, compared by some to Arizona's Grand Canyon, is found on Kauai. From there one can go by boat up the Wailua River, along whose banks the kings and nobles of the island lie buried, to the quiet and majestic Fern Grotto.

In some of the smaller towns on the neighbor islands there is also a leisurely charm. Hilo, the second biggest city in the islands, has fewer than 25,000 people. Japanese women walk with parasols through the rains in Hilo, and sampan buses, converted old limousines with seats along the sides and an overhanging top, provide the major transportation in the area. Kailua-Kona, on the Big Island, remains one of the loveliest and most relaxing of spots, with deep-sea fishing at its best in this area. Here was once the capital of Hawaii under Kamehameha I and Liholiho. Nearby are many historic relics of the Hawaiian past as well as Captain Cook's monument. Lahaina, on Maui, once the center of the big whaling operations on the islands, is now a plantation town. But it still has many buildings and churches left over from the old days and preserves a sleepy, nineteenth-century atmosphere.

Most of the tourists who come to the outer islands for any length of time are actually knowledgeable people from Honolulu out for a quiet vacation or a week end away from the city. Mainland tourists when they visit the neighbor islands at all do so too quickly to savor their flavor. While it is claimed that the outer islands lack the facilities to accommodate large numbers of tourists, many of their hotels have vacancies a good part of the time. As Waikiki becomes increasingly crowded, more mainland visitors will discover the neighbor islands. American Factors, one of the Big Five companies, and other interests have begun to plan new hotels and other tourist facilities there.

These islands, especially Maui, Hawaii, and Kauai, have the possibilities for a flourishing tourist business. They also have the resources for developing farming and light industry. If Hawaii is to develop in the sustained and balanced way the planners hope, its growth will have to include the neighbor islands.

8. *At Last—the Fiftieth State*

What does Hawaii expect to get out of statehood? Perhaps the question ought to be reversed: What will the United States get out of Hawaii's statehood? For the truth is that Hawaii is not likely to get some of the tangible rewards that have in the past accrued to new states. The intensity with which Hawaii campaigned for statehood in recent years had little to do with any expectation of immediate advantage.

When I asked William F. Quinn, Hawaii's last appointed and first elected governor, what he foresaw in the way of statehood's economic impact, the first thing he mentioned was that it would cost $400,000 more a year in services and salaries which Hawaii would have to furnish for itself. He did not see this as a very important problem — one half of one percent of Hawaii's annual budget. He brought it up to emphasize that Hawaii was self-sufficient as a state, well able to support itself without special federal aid.

Quinn did add that there would be certain economic advantages from statehood. Federal grants for roads and for some programs of the Department of Health, Education and Welfare are computed more favorably for states than for territories. Statehood may help promote further mainland investment, which has already been coming along at an ever-increasing rate. Representa-

Once occupied by Queen Liliuokalani, this mansion, called Washington Place, is the official residence of Hawaii's governors

tives of the New York bond market have testified at congressional hearings that hitherto they have regarded Hawaii as a foreign market.

George Mason, director of the Economic Planning and Co-ordination Authority, noted that many suppliers of goods to Hawaii classed it as an "export" market and charged higher rates which may now come down somewhat. But he added that the principal impact will be "psychological." There will be greater interest in Hawaii on the part of mainland investors, businessmen, and tourists.

Business leaders whom I asked about statehood had much the same viewpoint. They thought it was a good thing, but certainly did not expect the same substantial benefits from statehood as did

More than a century ago King Kamehameha III was intrigued by the statehood idea

their counterparts in Alaska. Hawaiian sugar has long enjoyed the same position as sugar produced on the mainland, and this situation is not expected to change one way or the other.

Union spokesmen said, "It really won't have much effect on our membership. We won't get anything out of statehood. We campaigned for it ever since World War II because we thought it would be a good thing for Hawaii and the United States."

The truth is that most people in Hawaii wanted statehood — seventeen to one in the June 1959 referendum after Congress finally approved Hawaii's admission to the Union — because they regarded it as their democratic right and not because they expected some federal handout.

They wanted it all the more because it has been so long deferred, more than one hundred years after the issue was first raised in Washington by expansionist congressmen and in Hawaii by King Kamehameha III, who saw statehood as a means of stabilizing his regime against internal opposition and the threat of raids by mainland adventurers. For more than fifty years statehood has been the dream of responsible people in Hawaii. In fact, this was the dream of the Yankees who overthrew the monarchy.

But they felt it was a dream rather than a practical possibility. Resolutions memorializing Congress on behalf of statehood became a ritual in the territorial legislature. One member of the legislature, introducing such a proposal in 1915, admonished his colleagues: "Let no member of the House treat the resolution memorializing Congress as a joke." The idea seemed unrealistic because there was always one major obstacle, the same obstacle that blocked statehood up to 1959. This was Hawaii's predominantly nonwhite population. When Hawaii's Japanese population reached forty-two percent of the total during the 1920's, members of Congress shuddered at the "yellow menace" and wouldn't even hear about statehood. Some of them still shudder, but their colleagues in 1959 voted them down – and by a convincing four to one majority.

By this time, another old argument, Hawaii's noncontiguity with the mainland, has been made almost irrelevant by the airplane.

It was during the 1930's that statehood became a very serious matter to important people in Hawaii. Statehood seemed to them the answer to a series of dramatic challenges to the *status quo* there. These forces were brought to the surface, strangely enough, by a sensational murder case. Mrs. Thalia Massie, wife of a young Navy officer, charged in September 1931 that she was raped and beaten by a group of young Hawaiians and Japanese. The lurid trial made headlines on the mainland, and aroused fears about the supposed lawlessness of Hawaii's non-Caucasian population. When a jury failed to agree on a verdict, Mrs. Massie's husband and mother killed one of the defendants. Although convicted of manslaughter, they were freed within an hour by Governor Lawrence M. Judd. Now the local population was furious and charged Navy pressure on the governor.

As a result of all the excitement about the case, a federal investigation of crime in Hawaii was launched. The hearings became a forum for attacks on the Big Five – and for a blast at the islands' Orientals by Rear Admiral Stirling. He questioned the loyalty of Hawaii's Japanese, said that a "disturbing intermixture of races" was producing "types of a lower moral and mental caliber" and urged a government "by men primarily of the Caucasian race." Stirling's solution was a commission type of government, appointed from Washington and with strong military representation. The idea had high-placed support in the capital, but made the kamaainas shudder.

As if this were not bad enough, the old order faced a threat from a different direction. President Franklin D. Roosevelt sponsored a bill for the appointment of a nonresident governor "who will be absolutely impartial in his decisions on matters as to which there may be a difference of local opinion." This was a barely disguised thrust at the kamaainas, and the old-timers had frightening visions of Fiorello H. LaGuardia or some other "wild-eyed radical" being sent in as governor.

Even more serious was the passage of the Jones-Costigan amendment to the Agricultural Adjustment Act, setting up the methods of sugar control, under which Hawaii was classified as a "foreign" area along with Cuba, Puerto Rico, and the Philippines. Quotas announced in 1934 cut mainland imports of sugar from Hawaii and imposed restrictions on sugar from the islands that did not apply to the mainland.

It was at this point that the sugar interests of Hawaii, which on the whole had been rather cool to statehood, suddenly decided that here was the answer. Statehood would remove the discriminations against sugar and would eliminate the threat of outside control from any source. Many public-spirited citizens, such as the late delegate to Congress, Victor S. K. Huston, had been statehood partisans well before this. But an active campaign for statehood dates from about the middle 1930's.

Campaigning directly on the statehood issue, Samuel Wilder King was elected delegate in November 1934 with substantial business support. King's first act as delegate, on January 7, 1935, was to introduce a statehood bill.

The legislature set up a commission to work for statehood, and together with local business groups helped finance a visit by a

The Judiciary Building, back view – in Honolulu's civic center

joint congressional committee, the first of many to investigate Hawaii's fitness for statehood. At the ensuing hearings there was testimony favoring statehood from the islands' economic and political leaders. Some opposition spokesmen expressed fears that statehood might tighten Big Five control, and some raised questions about the loyalty of the Japanese which obviously troubled members of the congressional committee. The committee recommended that statehood be "deferred" for further consideration "after determination of the sentiment" of the people of Hawaii. Representative John Rankin of Mississippi dissented with the stronger view that it be "indefinitely postponed."

This was less than the statehood advocates wanted, but the situation was far from hopeless. The statehood forces picked up the challenge to test local sentiment by setting a plebiscite in 1940 and by launching a publicity campaign to sell both the people of Hawaii and the mainland on the idea of statehood. The plebiscite showed a two-to-one vote for statehood.

World War II put a temporary quietus on the statehood campaign. Although Delegate Joseph R. Farrington introduced a statehood bill in 1943, it was shunted aside. But after the war the statehood drive resumed in earnest. The legislature appropriated $100,000 to bring more congressmen to Hawaii, and they came in droves. The statehood commission estimated that between 1937 and 1959 there were twenty hearings on statehood, covering everything from agriculture to Hawaii's war record. The hearings heard 378 witnesses in 6,500 pages of printed testimony.

Out of all the testimony there could only emerge the fact that Hawaii was a modern American community completely prepared for statehood. Its immigrants had become citizens. New generations were born in Hawaii. They took themselves seriously as Americans; their record on registration and voting was better than in most states.

A long period of self-government had amply prepared Hawaii for the responsibilities of statehood. Its bicameral legislature worked smoothly, although there were complaints until recently that the House of Representatives as well as the Senate were weighted in favor of the outer islands. Its major islands were governed by elected county officials, and there was also effective city-county government in Honolulu, Hilo, and other larger communities. In 1950, anticipating eventual statehood, Hawaii adopted by referendum vote a state constitution which is considered as modern and efficient as any in the United States. Indeed, Hawaii's government is considered in some respects more efficient than in most states. The state government has a larger role than in most areas, co-ordinating education, welfare, and other services, supervising even police and liquor control, and eliminating the waste of overlapping and overgrown local and county government. Missing only was the right to elect its own governor and its representatives in Congress.

Moreover, the congressional investigations repeatedly showed that Hawaii was almost completely united behind statehood. True, a few of the older residents were a bit apprehensive about the Japanese. But they were distinctly a minority, even in their own circles. Hawaiian business interests continued to support statehood, and now there came a stronger support from the various racial groups which had begun to participate more actively in politics and from all segments of the labor movement.

On the mainland, too, sentiment for statehood kept mounting. Shortly after World War II, Secretary of the Interior Harold Ickes and President Harry Truman, their doubts apparently dispelled by the war record of Hawaii's Japanese, endorsed the cause. Both Democratic and Republican national conventions swung into line. President Eisenhower made eloquent statements for statehood. Military spokesmen, their earlier fears proven groundless, added support; among those speaking up favorably were Admiral Chester Nimitz and General Douglas MacArthur. All kinds of national organizations – from the Protestant Episcopal Church of America to the American Water Works Association – came out for statehood. The House of Representatives passed statehood bills in 1947, 1950, and 1953, and the Senate in 1954 passed a combined Hawaii-Alaska statehood bill. The State Department in 1955 said statehood "would serve to support American foreign policy and strengthen the position of the United States in international relations." A Gallup poll in 1958 showed mainland public opinion nine to one for statehood.

What then was holding up statehood? The opposition of a formidable and influential Southern bloc in Congress was undoubtedly a major factor, and occasionally its members spoke out frankly. Representative Howard Smith of Virginia has said with unmistakable clarity, "One chinaman in Hawaii would have the same power in the election of Senators to the Senate of the United States as 31 Americans of the great state of New York." On March 12, 1959, the day the House passed the statehood bill, Representative James C. Davis of Georgia told his colleagues, "The question of the population in Hawaii, I think, is a very serious one. The population is predominantly Oriental." Stating (erroneously) that "82 percent of the people of Hawaii come from an oriental background," Senator George Smathers of Florida declared that we cannot admit Hawaii to the Union and "still protect things in which we who love the United States believe.

Nor can we do so and still maintain the high standard of living or the purity of our democracy."

By 1959 it was no longer considered good form to raise the race issue too blatantly, and it was soft-pedaled in the final debates. It was the Communist argument which loomed large against statehood. Put in a nutshell, it was that the International Longshoremen's & Warehousemen's Union controls Hawaii and that the Communists control the ILWU. Senator James O. Eastland of Mississippi said that "the Communist world conspiracy . . . will be served by the grant of statehood to Hawaii." If Hawaii is made a state, said Senator John C. Stennis of Mississippi, "the rising tide of Asiatic Communism will have a direct route to the Senate of the United States with two votes." Representative John Pillion of New York said that by approving statehood "we actually invite two Soviet agents to take seats in the United States Senate."

This argument must have caused some rather wry laughter in the board rooms of the Big Five companies. For in past years radical critics of the sugar interests in Hawaii have repeatedly charged that statehood was an invention of the Big Five intended to tighten their control over Hawaii and to enhance their influence in Washington.

In its issue of March 14, 1959, *Business Week* suggested that the Communist issue, originally brought up against the ILWU in the 1949 strike and other labor disputes, boomeranged against the groups which raised it. Noting that the Big Five had at one time been opposed to statehood and in recent years have been overwhelmingly for it, *Business Week* said:

> "It was not the direct opposition of the Big Five, however, that delayed statehood so long. It was the indirect result of their fight against organization of Hawaii's workers when the unions started moving in after the war.
>
> "To fight the unions, large employers hammered away at charges that labor leaders were largely Communists, and they built up the Communist menace so zealously that the issue blocked statehood for years.
>
> "Today, businessmen will concede that the Communist influence of even Harry Bridges' International Longshoremen's & Warehousemen's Union was exaggerated. The FBI's last count puts the number of Communists in Hawaii at around 25."

Congressmen, on one of many investigating tours to Hawaii, are shown here meeting with ILWU leaders

To those unfamiliar with the facts, the Communist issue picked up by Senator Eastland and others seemed impressive. But among the facts were Hawaii's casualty lists in the Korean War, which happened to be more than four times bigger than the average for the United States. Hawaii's troops distinguished themselves in Korea, and the *Honolulu Star-Bulletin* ran three pages of casualties as an answer to Eastland's assertion that Hawaii was a "Communist community." Hawaii did not seem about to become a Soviet naval base.

In the end, the facts caught up with the opposition to statehood. In 1958 Representative J. Arthur Younger, a California Republican, suggested that some of the congressional ballyhoo about communism "may be a smokescreen for racial prejudice." A similar conclusion was reached after an on-the-spot survey by a group of representatives and senators headed by Representative Leo W. O'Brien, New York Democrat and chairman of the House Committee on Interior and Insular Affairs.

Gradually many in Hawaii and in Congress began to believe that Eastland and his group were doing far more to aid Communist propaganda than any Communists, real or alleged, in

Symbolic of the unique background of the new state is this statue of King Kamehameha I in Honolulu's civic center

Hawaii. In the world of the 1950's racism in the South had become a major liability for the United States, and the racial democracy practiced in Hawaii had become a major asset.

As the opposition began to weaken, Delegate John A. Burns took over the strategy in Congress for the final statehood push. He made what seemed to some a costly compromise. He broke a congressional deadlock in 1958 by agreeing to let Alaska get statehood ahead of Hawaii.

For this, said a *New York Times* dispatch from Honolulu, he was branded at the time "little short of a traitor." But, the *Times* added, "now the islanders have seen his tactical move pay off." With Alaska in the Union, as it deserved to be, there was hardly an argument for keeping out Hawaii, which is at least as accessible to the main centers of the continental United States, which

Vice-President Richard M. Nixon welcoming Senator-elect Hiram L. Fong and his wife to Washington. Mr. Fong is the first person of Chinese descent elected to the U. S. Senate

has a bigger population, a more stable economy, and will require less federal aid.

The final vote was decisive enough, 76 to 15 in the Senate, 323 to 89 in the House, with the opposition consisting mainly of congressmen from the deep South.

The argument that swayed many in Congress and elsewhere to support statehood was expressed among others by Senator Henry Jackson of Washington:

> "In admitting Hawaii to the Union, we shall get more perhaps than we give. It has always been our desire, however skeptically others may have regarded us in the past, to live upon terms of peace, amity, and active co-operation with the great Asian peoples. . . . And I think we may come the closer to it as Hawaii becomes a part of the Union, as Asians see that we do mean what we say and do say what we mean."

Hawaii has, in fact, given to Asia and the world a meaningful demonstration of democracy in action. In its first state election, in the summer of 1959, it chose a capable and experienced team representative of its people, regardless of color and race. As United States Senators it elected Hiram L. Fong, a leading Chinese-American businessman, and Oren E. Long, a Kansas-born educator and social worker who first came to Hawaii in 1917 and won appointments as superintendent of public instruction and governor. Hawaii's first member of the House is Daniel K. Inouye, a wounded, much-decorated, one-armed veteran of the 442nd Infantry, who is typical of the whole generation of young Japanese-Americans who fought with such gallantry in World War II. William F. Quinn, an energetic Irish-American lawyer born in Rochester, New York, won out as governor against strong opposition from John A. Burns, Hawaii's top Democrat, who was supported by the ILWU. Fong and Quinn are Republicans. Long and Inouye are Democrats. No single party or union or racial bloc was dominant. But if the election confirmed the fears of some Southerners that men of Asian ancestry would be elected, it also upheld the hopes of most people in Hawaii and of most members of Congress. Democracy works in our new state.

9. The Immigrant Epic

There is under way in Hawaii a repetition of the great immigrant epic which unfolded earlier on the mainland where Irish, Germans, Jews, Czechs, Poles, Italians, and a score of other nationalities, emerging from the garment shops and the coal mines and the steel mills, achieved education and success. It is now accepted as a truism that the millions of European immigrants helped make America great and became in every sense an integrated part of the nation. Although it is not so generally known, the story of the Oriental immigrants to Hawaii is almost identical. They have become educated and Americanized. They have become part of America, contributed to it and built it.

> "When my grandfather came over in 1875, it took him 65 days on the boat from China. He was brought over a contract laborer on a sugar plantation. Then he managed to save enough to buy out his contract. He bought a little land and went into rice farming."

The tall, rangy man reaches into an expensive attaché case and hands me a mimeographed biographical sheet which begins: "Chinn Ho – Age 55 – Investment Banker." Then he sits back comfortably behind his desk on the sixth floor of the Capital Investment Company and continues with his story. He talks easily. A polka-dot bow tie adds a dash of color and informality to his dark business suit.

Many Chinese and Japanese immigrants took to rice farming as their first step off the plantation

While he is talking, I glance hastily down the mimeographed sheet. It has all the essential facts about directorships and club memberships. It makes clear what I had already known — that Chinn Ho is one of the big men of Hawaii. But it rarely suggests the real story of Chinn Ho's rise up the economic ladder.

For all his efforts to become independent of plantation labor, his grandfather had had a hard time of it as a farmer. "My father became a small merchant, but he didn't make out too well. When I graduated high school in 1924, the family was not well off. My first job was selling novelties. But I went to the university at night, taking extension courses."

Then came a modest job with the Bishop Bank. Finance began to fascinate him. He went on to a job with a leading brokerage house, but felt he was being held down. Finally in 1944 he founded his own investment firm. The little biography fills in details. Chinn Ho is now president of nine companies of which

In the early 1900's water buffalos – now seldom seen in Hawaii – were brought from the Orient and used on the rice farms

Capital Investment is the most important. He is deeply involved in major real estate developments in Hawaii and California and in cattle ranching; he is a director of Hawaiian Airlines, Seaboard Finance of Hawaii, and the Honolulu Rapid Transit Company. He is president of the Bishop Museum Association, past president of the Commercial Club and the Honolulu Stock Exchange, an important figure in the Hawaii Visitors Bureau and the Red Cross.

Unlike Ben Dillingham's grandfather and the other grandfathers and great-grandfathers of the well-established Haole families, Chinn Ho's grandfather did not strike it rich at first. There was a long climb upward for the Ho family, and it took the third generation to make it. This is generally typical of those immigrant Japanese and Chinese families which are now in the front ranks of Hawaii's political and economic life.

Sometimes, but not often, the ascent was swifter. A full-page advertisement in the statehood edition of the *Honolulu Star-Bulletin* was headlined, "An American Dream Comes True," and featured photographs of an elderly Japanese couple and their grown children. It began with this paragraph:

> "The Zenpan Arakawa story is an American success story. It tells how a dauntless youth, granted the freedom to succeed in a land where opportunity abounds, rose from a humble beginning as a cane-field 'water boy,' nurtured a diminutive rural tailor shop and with ingenuity and friendly neighborliness developed it into Hawaii's largest department store outside of Honolulu."

The prose may sound a little ornate. But Arakawa did come to Hawaii in 1906, a slender boy of 19 who didn't take to the work in the cane fields. He started making clothes for the field hands in a little tailor shop at Waipahu, not far from Pearl Harbor, which has since grown into a very successful family enterprise.

Of course, not all of the almost five hundred thousand plantation laborers imported to work in Hawaii's sugar and pineapple fields rose from rags to riches. Not all were Oriental Horatio Algers. Far from it! Tens of thousands lived and died on the plantations, earning just enough with hard work for the barest necessities. Other tens of thousands returned home to China, Japan, or the Philippines – not much better off than when they came. Many thousands went on to the mainland in search of opportunity. But many who were not ambitious for themselves and knew they could not overcome the barriers of poverty and race and low status in their own lifetimes helped their children and their grandchildren up the economic ladder.

The Chinese, who were the first large group of immigrant workers brought to Hawaii, were also the first to start leaving the plantations. Many bought little farms of their own. But the general trend was to Honolulu where they set up small businesses. The Chinese in Hawaii are now a predominantly urban people – more than seventy percent of Hawaii's 35,000 Chinese live in Honolulu. Together with urbanization came economic advancement, which has been particularly rapid since World War II. In

Few women were brought in during the years of the great Filipino immigration. Here is one wearing a dress costume

1950 only about five percent of Hawaii's employed Chinese were listed as plantation laborers, and the percentage is probably even lower a decade later. More than thirty percent of the Chinese were classified as managers, officials, and proprietors and as professional and technical workers. While charts and statistics do not tell the whole story, the figures show the Chinese as only slightly behind the Caucasians in their status on the occupational ladder. Chinese capital is now a considerable factor in banks, real estate, and airline companies.

The story of the other immigrant groups is similar, differing only in the timing and degree of the rise. The Japanese came later and in greater numbers; hence they have come up later and somewhat more slowly. But the trend has been unmistakable, and recent progress has been spectacular. In 1940 almost half the employed Japanese in Hawaii were classified as unskilled; ten years later only a quarter of the Japanese were in this category.

A young serviceman of Filipino extraction

In 1920 there were only 25,000 Japanese in Honolulu; by 1950 there were 92,000. While the number of Japanese plantation workers is second only to the Filipinos, they are no longer primarily a rural plantation people. They have risen in the skilled trades, in the professions, in business and politics. There are now Japanese university professors, agricultural experts, judges. They are a major and respected part of the life of Hawaii.

As the last major group of immigrants, the Filipinos have stayed on the plantations later and have come up more slowly. They have also had special problems in adaptation. Perhaps the most acute of these is that the majority of Filipinos brought in were single men without families. This led to lonely and abnormal lives on the plantations, and to some of the gambling and drinking and cock-fighting with which they have been charged. About half of Hawaii's plantation workers today are Filipinos. Although about 120,000 Filipinos were brought in between 1906 and 1930, they did not increase as rapidly as other groups in the popula-

Americanized Korean girls in Honolulu wearing their national costumes

tion because most of them were single men. Moreover, a good many of them continued to look on the Philippine Islands as their homeland and eventually returned there.

The Filipinos are still predominantly a rural people in Hawaii. They are still close to the bottom of the ladder. In Honolulu many of them still live in the more depressed areas. But the same general upward trends are now apparent among the Filipinos too. Urbanization increased rapidly among them during World War II; they have also begun to move up economically, sending their children to college, entering the professions and business.

Hawaii is often described at the University of Hawaii as "a great social laboratory." And the experience of Hawaii has disproved old myths and shibboleths about unbridgeable racial differences between Asians and Caucasians. Cultural backgrounds

Some Hawaiian women still practice old handicrafts. This woman is weaving hats and purses from lauhala or pandanus leaves

rather than race have proved decisive in the adjustment of the different national groups in Hawaii. For example, Caucasian Portuguese and Puerto Rican immigrants with more of a peasant background have left the plantations more slowly than Korean and Chinese immigrants with more of an urban and mercantile tradition.

One of the sad paradoxes is that the Hawaiians and part-Hawaiians, descendants of the original inhabitants of the islands, are still among the depressed section of population. Actually there are very few pure Hawaiians left – perhaps 10,000 in all Hawaii. But the part-Hawaiians are now the fastest growing part of the population, about twenty percent of the total in 1959. The original trend toward biological extinction after the initial contact with the white men began to be reversed about 1920 when the number of part-Hawaiians began increasing, at first slowly and now ever more rapidly. The Hawaiians and part-Hawaiians have not, however, moved up socially and economically in proportion to their number. There are a few Hawaiians and Caucasian-Hawaiians at

Some Hawaiians and part-Hawaiians work as entertainers

the upper reaches of society, but the greatest proportion of them are still engaged in unskilled labor. Certainly they do not play a major role in business life as do the Japanese and Chinese. In recent years the part-Hawaiians have started to make more progress. Quite a few have become lawyers and have achieved prominence in politics. But they still have a long way to go.

The reasons again are cultural rather than racial. "The whites were a commercial people," a well-educated Hawaiian woman explains. "So were the Orientals. But the Hawaiians were not. They had no sense of property, of private ownership, of business."

Dr. Andrew W. Lind, one of Hawaii's leading sociologists, put it to me this way, "It just isn't true that East and West don't meet. There is more in common between Occident and Orient than we realize. The peoples of Asia have many of the same values, the same emphasis on family, on education, on getting ahead that we do. But the Polynesians didn't have the same values, and the process of adjustment has been a more painful one."

East and West keep meeting all the time in Hawaii. The proc-

Leis, a gesture of affection for visitors, are made and sold by many Hawaiian women

ess is more obvious in Honolulu, more rapid among the younger generation. But it is also taking place on the plantations, particularly since World War II and the rise of trade-unionism as a force which has made the workers feel a sense of group identity extending beyond racial and national lines.

A few years ago a Japanese university student told the story of her mother in a paper written for one of her courses. It was the story of a Japanese picture bride who came from Okinawa in 1922 at the age of sixteen and over the years worked on the plantation, wove pandanus leaf hats, and raised chickens – in between raising ten children.

"In 1946," she says, "mother went back to work on the plantation and has been working steady since. Her wages are now $200 a month, many times more than in her early days. She had to go back to work in order to send us all to school because dad's meager earnings alone, a result of his failing health . . . , were not enough. At this time, there are seven of us in school – four in

The University of Hawaii — a goal for Hawaii's young people of all national backgrounds

grammar school, one in high school, one in business school and one in the university. Mother has sacrificed a lot to provide her children with an education and is proud of the fact that she has never had any debts to pay."

The daughter recalls that her mother started taking adult education classes in English two or three nights a week during World War II. "Just recently, mother took the greatest step thus far toward Americanization. She began attending classes which prepare Japanese aliens for naturalization. . . . She has been studying the important phases of American history and government and finds that very interesting. As a result, she has taken more interest in politics. Mother has indeed progressed in a great many ways toward becoming Americanized, and I am very proud of her."

The drive for education, which represents both Americanization and the pathway to economic success, is everywhere evident among Hawaii's immigrant peoples. Now it is asserting itself among the Filipinos, just as it did earlier among the Chinese and

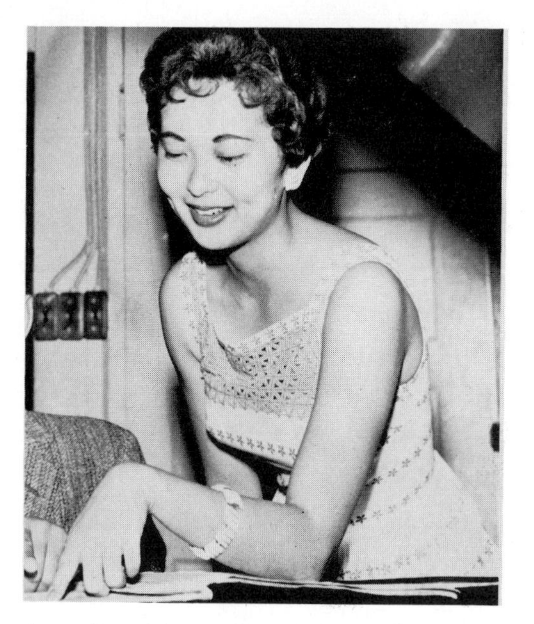

A student of mixed racial ancestry (the term "cosmopolitan" is now common in Hawaii) at the University

Japanese. I met one skilled Filipino worker earning perhaps $425 a month. Every month he sets aside a sum of $120 to send two sons to the university. Then he plans to send them to the mainland to professional schools so that one can become an engineer, the other a doctor.

The dream of even the poorest Oriental workers is to send their children to the university in Hawaii, and many do. Today almost ninety-five percent of Chinese and Japanese children, a higher percentage than among Caucasians, continue school beyond the compulsory age of sixteen. Three out of every five of Hawaii's high school graduates in 1958 were planning to continue their education. This is high by any standards. Hawaii boasts other significant statistics – such as the fact that ninety percent of registered voters actually go to the polls and that the percentage of citizenship among her Oriental peoples is now almost as high as among Caucasians. The immigrant peoples have become Americanized.

10. *Laboratory in Brotherhood*

How do the peoples of Hawaii really feel about each other? Do they get along as well as they are supposed to? Is there racial discrimination or bias? I asked these and similar questions everywhere in Hawaii, of government officials, school administrators, employers, men and women of all races and all walks of life.

"Are most of your friends Caucasians – or are there any Orientals who are part of your circle of friends?" I asked a vice-president of one of the Big Five companies.

"Many of my closest friends are Chinese and Japanese," he said. "There isn't any Haole exclusiveness among us. In fact, my four boys went out with Oriental girls. As it happens, they didn't marry them."

"Were you relieved?"

He paused a minute, then said, "As a matter of fact, I wasn't. There was one Chinese girl particularly that my oldest boy went around with that I was really fond of, a wonderful girl. And I was disappointed when he didn't marry her."

I put the same question in reverse to a leading Chinese businessman – whether any of his close friends are Caucasians.

"Very definitely," he said. "My social circle is mixed. The qualifications are economic rather than racial."

Usually, the answers I got were more generalized. But almost

A young Chinese girl in traditional costume

without exception men in Hawaii's public and business life assured me that there is no discrimination. Quite typical is a statement by Thomas Hitch, research director of the Hawaii Employers Council, "This heterogeneous mixture of people has learned to live together as a social whole better than any other mixed group in the world. While other parts of our nation are still torn by segregation issues, Hawaii offers a splendid example of racial harmony."

There is even a certain amount of competition as to who contributed most to this situation. While the ILWU claims credit for breaking down racial barriers and elevating the status of the Oriental peoples, employer spokesmen point to the role of the sugar industry in importing the Asian immigrants to begin with. Thus, HSPA has put out a chart, "Sugar's Role in Hawaii's Cosmopolitan Makeup," emphasizing that it was the sugar industry which brought hundreds of thousands of people from all over the world to work on the plantations.

A closer look suggests that the reality is more complex than the official picture. Everything is far from perfect in Hawaii. But Hawaii's image of itself is actually one of the factors making for co-operation among its people. It tries to live up to its reputation.

Hawaii still has problems, serious problems, in race relations. But they are of a different order from those to which we are accustomed on the mainland. When I asked the Big Five man about friendships and social relations, he discussed intermarriage. The kind of problem you get in Hawaii is whether it is socially acceptable for a top Haole executive to marry an Oriental woman. People will point to isolated pockets of what the Big Five vice-president referred to as "Haole exclusiveness," or to a few all-Caucasian clubs such as the Pacific Club and the Outrigger Canoe Club, or they will say that there are some top jobs in private industry which Hawaii's nonwhites feel are beyond their reach. In the circumstances of daily life affecting most people, Hawaii's reputation stands up quite well.

Of course, Hawaii's reputation as an interracial paradise has at times been oversold – with disillusioning results. Some mainland Negroes coming to Hawaii during and after World War II have been disappointed to find more discrimination than they expected. A study by the University of Hawaii concluded that this was "a carry-over from the continental United States" rather than an indigenous Hawaiian product. The conclusion is supported by the fact that there have long been many Negroes in Hawaii who did not encounter special problems – "black Portuguese." They came on whaling ships in the nineteenth century, settled down, and intermarried. The university's study also found that "local students are considerably more liberal regarding the American Negro than are mainland university students." Despite their small numbers, Negroes have been elected to public office in Hawaii.

For the most part Hawaii's achievements and problems in race relations are an outgrowth of its own peculiar history as a plantation area which imported workers from all over the world. Throwing these people together was bound to create some difficulties. There were, in fact, two major sources of friction – between the immigrant peoples themselves and between the immigrant workers as a whole and the Haoles.

Many of Asia's long-standing divisions and groupings and subgroupings were simply transported to Hawaii. For example, there were caste antagonisms between the Japanese from the home islands and those from Okinawa, who were considered inferior. There was friction between the middle-class Portuguese immigrants from the mother country and the peasant immigrants from the Azores and Madeira. Two groups of Filipino immigrants, the Visayans and the Tagalogs, tended to look down on a third group, the Ilocanos. Some of these differences continued until quite recently, with the Ilocanos sitting apart from the others in movie houses and Visayan parents frowning on dates between their children and young Ilocanos.

Similarly, there were certain points of friction between all the major groupings. As the last to come, the Filipinos had inferior economic and social status. All other groups looked down on the Puerto Ricans; many of the latter felt so sensitive about this that they described themselves as "Spanish." The Japanese on the whole tended to stick together and discouraged social mingling or intermarriage with other groups. Stereotypes developed about all the various nationalities in Hawaii, and you can still hear them occasionally. Haoles claimed that the Hawaiians were "lazy." Orientals said that the Haoles were "not clean" and didn't bathe often enough. It was said that the Japanese were "too pushy," and that the Chinese were "too commercial."

Haoles for the most part tended to consider the Orientals as inferior, and the Orientals and Hawaiians resented the Haoles. You can still hear expressions like "damn Haole." Anti-Haole feeling was, however, primarily economic rather than racial. The Hawaiians felt that the Haoles took the land, the Japanese and Chinese that the Haoles took all the good jobs.

In recent years the advances in race relations have been re-

A picnic of plantation workers

markable, and this applies to the plantations as well as Honolulu and other cities. While you still see signs like "Spanish camp" or "Chinese camp" in plantation communities, these are mainly vestiges of the past rather than indications of continuing segregation.

A Japanese girl from a plantation community describes the changes in her mother. "At first she was quite prejudiced against other racial groups," the daughter recalls. But now, "she realizes that in this world you have to be able to get along with all kinds of people of all races. She no longer reprimands her children for making friends with *gai-jin* (persons of other racial groups)."

I attended a union picnic of several hundred pineapple workers, mainly Filipino, Japanese, and part-Hawaiians. Dancing and games – including a rather original one in which teams competed in a live egg-throwing contest with rather messy consequences for the losers who broke the eggs – were completely interracial. Several Caucasian management representatives there with their families mingled easily with the plantation workers. There

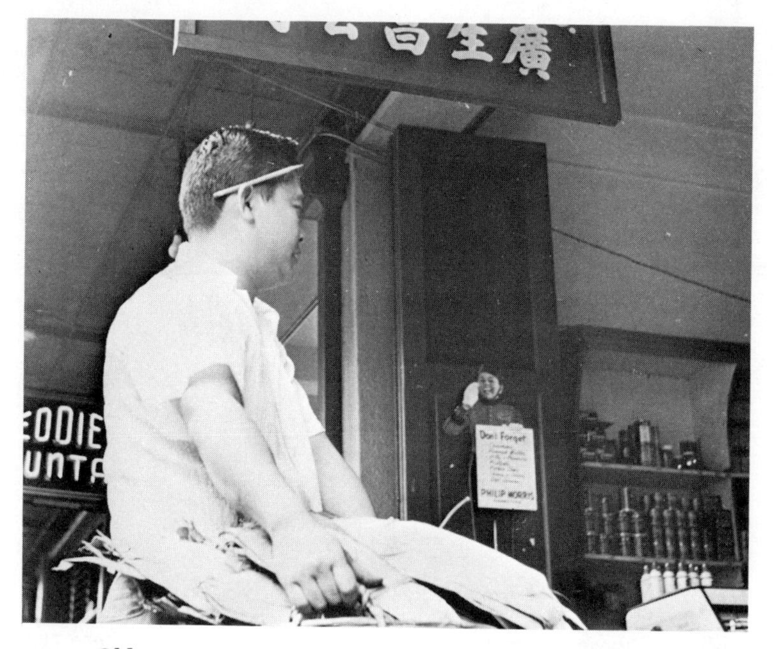

Old-country delicacies can still be bought in Chinatown

seemed genuinely friendly relations between the management people and the workers, relations free of obsequiousness on the part of the workers or of patronizing on the part of management.

The integration of Hawaii's peoples has taken place mainly in Honolulu, the largest center of population. And here the changes have been spectacular from the days when the immigrant workers started moving to the big city, clustering into their own little residential areas more or less according to race, into Chinatown, into Little Tokyos, Little Azores, Little Manilas, usually in the poorer, slum-ridden areas of town. The Japanese had a score of residential areas or "camps" within the city all with their own baths, Buddhist temples, shrines, tea houses, and language houses. But it should be said that housing segregation was never as rigidly enforced as on the mainland either by custom or restrictive covenant. Now the housing pattern is substantially interracial.

A choral group at Pauoa Elementary School

Most Chinese no longer live in Chinatown, although there are still old Chinese family association houses there as well as restaurants and shops. They started moving years ago into more exclusive areas, which received such names as "Chinese Hollywood" and "Mandarin Heights" and into racially mixed sections of the city. There are still a few areas of the city which are predominantly Japanese.

But generally speaking the trend has been toward housing integration – and segregation – on the basis of income. Middle-class suburban areas are fairly well mixed. It is only at the very top and the very bottom layers that there is, in effect, segregation. There are still a few exclusively Caucasian suburbs, and a few slum areas with poor homes and inadequate schools and other facilities, their population mainly Filipino and part-Hawaiian.

There is no segregation in Hawaii's public schools. But housing patterns, as on the mainland, have an effect on the schools. In low-income areas, where there are few Caucasians, the schools often have older, run-down buildings. There have also been two

There are no racial barriers here as children dance together

complicating factors, the language problem and the private schools.

Children from homes where Oriental languages were spoken often found difficulty in speaking English. Haoles and some more assimilated Oriental parents, on the other hand, were worried about the quality of the English spoken in the public schools where most of the children were Oriental. As a result, the English Standard Schools were set up in the 1920's as a part of the public school system. The entrance requirement was passing an oral English test. Actually, the schools were not segregated. By 1947 there were more Oriental children in the nine English Standard Schools than Haoles, and a quarter of the children were part-Hawaiian. But non-Caucasian parents felt that the schools tended to perpetuate the language liabilities of their children, and they are being eliminated.

Another oddity of the situation in Hawaii is the larger proportion of children attending private schools — 16 percent as against 11 percent on the mainland. These are mainly parochial schools maintained by the Catholic Church and by various Protestant denominations. Only one of the major private schools has been tinged with racial exclusiveness. This is Punahou, originally founded by the missionaries in 1841 to prevent the "contamination" of their children by Hawaiians.

While Punahou later accepted children of mixed marriages and nonmissionary Haole children, it did establish at the turn of the century an informal ten-percent quota on the number of Oriental children which was maintained until the 1940's. Much of the anti-Haole feeling in Hawaii has been directed at Punahou. In recent years racial barriers have been lowered. A Japanese boy has been president of the student body, and Orientals have been stars on its football team. It is an upper-class school with an excellent academic rating. Many wealthy Chinese send their children to Punahou, but the student body is still largely Caucasian.

The other major private school has long been known as "the Hawaiian school." This is Kamehameha Schools, with a truly magnificent plant, including boarding facilities, on Kapalama Heights overlooking Honolulu and its harbor. The school was founded by Princess Bernice Pauahi Bishop, last of the Kamehameha line and wife of Charles Reed Bishop who founded the Bishop National Bank. At her death in 1884, she left the income from her vast land holdings, about one ninth of the total land area of the islands, to the founding of a school for Hawaiian children. Income from the Bishop Estate, with more than 350,000 acres valued at about $30,000,000, goes entirely to the schools, accounting for their excellent dormitories, classrooms, shops, and gymnasiums. The Kamehameha Schools are considered among the best in Hawaii. But they have been a target for some of the feeling directed against the tight grip on island real estate maintained by a few of the old Hawaiian estates now managed largely by Haole financial interests. Originally designed for Hawaiian children, the school had to dilute its requirements to one half, one quarter, and now one eighth Hawaiian as the pure Hawaiian population declined.

One of the long-time bugaboos of Hawaii's race relations, and the one which has captured the most attention on the mainland, has been bloc voting. Especially when the Japanese population

Political campaigning with an Hawaiian flavor

came to more than forty percent of the population, fears were frequently expressed that they would control the elections – and this was used as a major argument against statehood. Now the population is so varied that it is obviously impossible for any one racial group to win on its own.

Dr. Andrew W. Lind, perhaps the leading student of Hawaii's peoples, contends flatly that "racial bloc voting, in the mainland sense of the rigorous control over an entire block of voters of a common race, does not occur in Hawaii, and even in the more restricted sense of voting exclusively for members of one's own ethnic group." From a study of the 1954 general election, John M. Digman of the University of Hawaii came to the somewhat more qualified conclusion, that "the chief determiner of the vote in elections" seems to be "voter preference for one party rather than the other." But he added that ethnic factors "are of considerable importance, and in a close election, could be decisive."

It may be that racial factors figure in elections. But the economic and political predilections of the voters obviously come first. Politicians, probably the best experts on voting trends, gave me numerous examples of elections in which Haole candidates ran well ahead of Japanese candidates in heavily populated Japanese districts, or where Chinese candidates won in non-Chinese districts. There are certain general trends among some of the racial groups. The Japanese tend to vote for Democrats, the Hawaiians and Caucasians for Republicans. But there are enough Democrats and Republicans in all racial groups to counteract political line-ups purely by race. Chinese, Japanese, Hawaiians, Portuguese, and many other nationalities have been elected on both party tickets. The bloc voting bugaboo has been pretty well laid to rest. Thus, in the state elections of July 1959, the proportion of offices won by nonwhites – forty-two out of eighty-one – was lower than their proportion in the population.

Job discrimination of the kind quite common on the mainland is almost unknown in Hawaii. Craftsmen or technicians or engineers or office workers of all races in Hawaii have no problems getting jobs in line with their skills. I heard no suggestion from Oriental spokesmen of the need for special legislation, such as fair employment practices commissions, that has been enacted in several other states. Where job problems still do exist they are at the upper reaches of finance and industry, which would not be affected by legislation in any case.

Even an informal or hasty visit to Castle & Cooke, C. Brewer & Company, the Bishop National Bank, or any of the other major old-line companies in Hawaii shows that non-Caucasian office workers, both men and women, are everywhere in evidence. Where complaints arise they come from Oriental executives who feel that limits have been placed on the levels to which they can rise in the Big Five companies.

A few years ago an employee of one of these companies told a University of Hawaii researcher, "I think there is some feeling among the directors and the officers that there may be certain repercussions if they were to promote an Oriental for the position of department head. By that I mean that the company is largely

Young women members of Teamsters Union paying dues

owned by the Haole interests and they might not like the idea of an Oriental telling them what to do and what should be their business program." While denying discrimination, a top Haole executive said much the same thing: "Actually, there is very little discrimination here in the islands. If Orientals are not in the top positions in this company it is because they would be unable to meet or entertain mainland business contracts."

There is still a feeling among some Orientals of frustration, of unfulfilled potential. I met a Chinese engineer who pulled out a list of about fifty of his colleagues, mainly Chinese, and said, "We have some of the ablest technical personnel in the world here in Hawaii. I would match them against mainland engineers from M.I.T. or any other school. But they're not getting their opportunity. Usually they're the number two men in their departments either in government or in business. They're not allowed to go to the top."

"What makes you say they're better than mainland personnel?" I asked. "Isn't that a sort of racism in reverse?"

"Well," he said, after a minute's pause, "We had to do it the

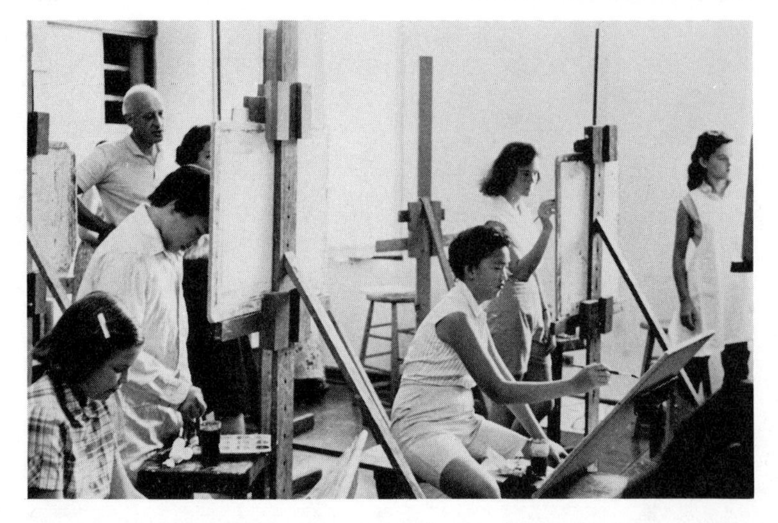

Young women painting at the Academy of Arts

hard way. We had to struggle for our education. We worked harder to get where we are, and now we feel that we're not being properly utilized."

Some Oriental experts and businessmen still find their best chances for advancement in firms owned by Chinese and Japanese capital. But gradually they are making headway both in private industry and government.

Even at the top levels of the old companies, racial barriers are slowly breaking down. One of Hawaii's major banks has added two Orientals to its board of directors. Other important companies are beginning to follow suit.

Some Orientals describe this as "window dressing." But it is a trend – and it may yet go further in the years ahead. A Japanese businessman told me he hesitated when he was asked to become a director of one of the leading companies. "I thought maybe I was being used as a front," he said. "But then I realized that there is a change in the thinking of some of these companies. There is a tendency toward integration socially and economically as well as politically."

As people live together in the same neighborhoods, work to-

Mother and child — a blending of races

gether in the same places of business, and as their children go together, close interracial friendships inevitably develop. These are not the exception in Hawaii. They are the rule; and they are perhaps the best index to the real state of race relations there.

Old lines between different castes and groups are disappearing. Navy personnel and their families have traditionally been a world of their own. But now departures from this pattern are more frequent. A Navy wife with several children was disappointed in her dream of Hawaii as a primitive Polynesian paradise. Bored with Navy life, she found herself "indulging in petty gossip and constant complaining," and finally decided to enroll at the university for something to do. There she met the real

Many racial strains produce happy results in these young Hawaiian women

Hawaii, the racially mixed and diverse Hawaii. She made new friends. "In general," she says, "I like my new picture of Hawaii far better than the one I had when I arrived. Less romantic perhaps, but surely more alive, more vital, more interesting."

At the university, some six hundred students of varied racial ancestry were asked to indicate the ethnic background of their five best friends. It turned out that 77.3 percent had close friends cutting across ethnic lines. The same group of students was asked to identify the racial background of their dates – and it turned out that almost half the students had dates with partners of different ethnic groups from their own.

Intermarriage is generally accepted in Hawaii. At first it was a matter of necessity. Many early sailors and merchants married Hawaiian women because there were no other. Single plantation workers often had to marry women of different racial groups if they were to get married at all. But now it is entirely a matter of choice. Intermarriage takes place simply because people of different races are thrown together and like each other. As the Navy wife quoted above says, "When I first arrived in Hawaii, interracial marriage seemed just as wrong to me as it does to most mainlanders; however, after my association with the girls of other races on campus, I now wonder what all the fuss is about."

Interracial marriages are as successful in Hawaii as any other kind. Family and group pressures which might make difficulties are gradually disappearing. The results of intermarriage have hardly confirmed the dire prophets, like Admiral Stirling, who predicted a physically and mentally inferior people from racial mingling. Children of mixed marriages have stood up as well as anybody else to competition in school and on the job. Their physical appearance is one of the things that impresses visitors most favorably. Many of Hawaii's strikingly beautiful women and handsome men are the products of intermarriage.

President Eisenhower referred to Hawaii as "a unique example of a community in a successful laboratory in human brotherhood." It is a human laboratory, and it is therefore far from perfect. But I know of few places in the world where so many peoples of different races and nationalities have managed to live so well together.

11. Unity in Diversity

A university professor, studying the cultural effects of the mixing and blending of Hawaii's diverse peoples, tells the story of a Chinese-Hawaiian family with six girls and one boy.

> "Five of the girls are married, respectively to a Chinese, a Japanese-Hawaiian, a Chinese-Hawaiian, a Japanese and Filipino husband, each with the approval of the parents. There are frequent occasions when the whole family happily gathers at the parental home. In this family the Oriental influence is seen in the emphasis on the family's integrity and good name. The children were encouraged to seek education and were kept under control by the formula, 'You must not bring the family into bad repute. What will people say?' As the children started earning they contributed to the family income. The Hawaiian influence is seen in the fact that both parents speak Hawaiian and have taught a little of the language to the family. The influence of the West is seen in their religion – they are Catholics – and in their acceptance of the American way of life."

In microcosm this family is Hawaii today. I don't mean that this is an average family. There is probably no such thing in Hawaii. The Hawaiian influence, for example, is unusually strong in this case. But the family is typical both of the interracial marriages so common in Hawaii and of the interaction of the dif-

An Hawaii family of mixed racial strains enjoys a luau in its back yard

ferent cultural influences in the community.

It was inevitable that the diverse languages, traditions, and cultures in Hawaii should interact on one another. This has been taking place for a long time. What is new is the growing recognition by many people, by the press, public officials, and the school system that this process, far from being un-American, is beneficial both to Hawaii and to America.

Thousands of second- and third-generation Japanese and Chinese in Hawaii believe that the process of Americanization proceeded too heedlessly, too thoughtlessly, too swiftly. They are joined by a great many Caucasians – educators, professionals in the fields of art and culture, and just plain citizens – who feel that all Hawaii has been losing something as a result of undiscriminating Americanization. A genuine effort is now taking place to reverse this process or at least to slow it up, and there is still sufficient cultural diversity left to make this far from a futile effort.

Some of the interest in reviving or maintaining the component parts of Hawaii's multinational and multiracial culture is undoubtedly commercial or political in origin. Hawaii's attractiveness to tourists depends in part on its uniqueness, and particularly on the appeal of old Hawaiian songs, dances, and customs. This has been a factor in the efforts to revive Hawaiian culture, often in synthetic or vulgarized form. The new importance of the Far East in American foreign relations has similarly stimulated efforts to maintain the rapidly waning knowledge among Hawaii's Oriental peoples of the Chinese, Korean, and Japanese language and traditions. But much of the interest seems to be due simply to a realization that Hawaii will be a richer and more interesting place to live in if its culture is not altogether standardized and "Americanized" by television, radio, movies, and popular magazines.

The process of Americanization began in some ways more than a century ago and affected the Hawaiians first of all. The total impact of the missionary influence was one of Americanization, not only in religion but in the over-all way of life. Missionary influence discouraged many aspects of Hawaiian culture. An obvious example was missionary disapproval of the hula, which has been called the opera of old Hawaii because musicians, dancers, and singers joined to perform religious rites or to narrate history and old folk tales. Missionaries got the dancers, dressed at first only in tapa skirts and flower leis, into cotton dresses and later middy blouses and full skirts. Eventually the hulas were banned, and by the time King Kalakaua tried to revive them in the 1880's there were not too many Hawaiians left who knew the old dances and chants.

The hula, of course, now enjoys a continuing vogue. There are many dancing schools where island youngsters of all nationalities are taught the hula, and no tourist can escape grass-skirted dances at luaus and Hawaiian feasts staged by the big Waikiki hotels. Many of the older Hawaiians frown on the current hula as a crude imitation. Mrs. Jennie Wilson, who once danced at the royal court in Honolulu, says, "These so-called hulas are nothing like the real thing, and most of the entertainers dancing hulas have been brought in from Samoa." On the other hand, there have been noncommercial efforts both by Hawaiians and Caucasians

Hulas are still popular with the younger generation

to revive authentic old dances and chants.

Decline of the Hawaiian language cannot be blamed on the missionaries. In fact, they devised an alphabet and taught the Hawaiians to read and write their own language. This made it possible for Hawaiian writers and scholars, of whom the best known are Malo, Kepelino, Kamakau, and Haleole, to preserve the tales and legends of their people. But as English became the language of commerce and trade, the mark of culture and wealth, some of the chiefs and kings themselves discouraged use of the Hawaiian language. The pressure for Americanization came until fairly recently from upper-class Hawaiians who wanted to slough off as rapidly as possible the old language and the old ways.

"We were punished for speaking Hawaiian," says Mrs. Mary

Some old-timers frown on commercialized hula shows, such as this one at the International Market Place at Waikiki

Pukui of those days. Mrs. Pukui, a scholar at the Bishop Museum, has been working on authoritative Hawaiian dictionaries and has been collecting the old folk sayings and stories. She reports some revival in knowledge of the Hawaiian language. The Kamehameha Schools teach at least a rudimentary knowledge of Hawaiian, and the language has been introduced in the high schools.

On Niihau Island, smallest of the Hawaiian island chain, the wealthy Robinson family has maintained a sanctuary of the old Hawaii. Only pure Hawaiians live on Niihau – and strangers are discouraged. A Japanese fighter pilot in World War II discovered this to his chagrin. He tried to trick Benjamin Kanahale, a local Hawaiian, into helping him. Although Kanahale did not know about the war, he soon gathered that something was wrong, turned on the armed Japanese, and, although wounded three times, overpowered him and smashed his head against a lava wall.

Primitive Hawaiian instruments are still used occasionally at public entertainments. Musicians pound hollowed bamboo of various lengths on a spread on the ground, producing an organlike effect

Niihau's reaction to friendly outsiders is less violent, but they are not permitted without specific permission of the Robinson family. The Hawaiians work on the Robinson ranch, eat fish and poi as of old, have long luaus on the beach, and speak their ancient language. Babies are still delivered by Hawaiian midwives. There are no electric lights, no radio or TV – and no whiskey, or even beer or soft drinks. But the very isolation which has successfully preserved the Niihau colony has deprived it of any influence on the rest of Hawaii.

It is questionable whether, even with synthetic encouragement, the Hawaiian language and culture will long survive as independent entities. The last Hawaiian newspaper in Honolulu was published in 1927, although a newspaper in Hilo kept struggling until World War II. But the Hawaiian influence on the general culture

Young Hawaiians re-enact a scene out of the past, wearing feather garments from the Bishop Museum collection. At left and right are kahilis, feather standards carried before chiefs and denoting high ranks

is considerable. It is felt in the innumerable Hawaiian place names, in phrases and words which have filtered into the language, perhaps in the intangibles of pervasive attitudes and way of life. One can get into arguments over whether Hawaii's "aloha spirit" is something more than a tourist attraction, or whether the somewhat slower pace of life is due to the weather or the Hawaiian influence. But there is no doubt that the Hawaiian element is part of the culture, tradition, and history of the new state.

Oriental languages and cultures are, of course, a vital and continuing part of Hawaii's life. The older generation of immigrants generally tended to cling to old ways, despite exhortations to Americanize. Some of the older people still wear traditional Chinese and Japanese dress. Their influence is seen in the large number of Buddhist temples throughout Hawaii. There are still Chinese family association houses where joss sticks are burned at shrines in honor of the departed dead; leaving one of

Japanese *bon* dancing is a popular summer event in Hawaii

them, I saw a group of Chinese boys in baseball uniforms getting into a truck. But now it is among many of the younger generation, who had earlier tended to break with the old, that a reappraisal of their heritage is taking place.

Nelson Doi, the young state senator from the Big Island, is one of many Chinese and Japanese in Hawaii who told me of the change in their own attitudes within the last few years.

"When I was a boy growing up on the Big Island," he says, "our parents made us all go to Japanese language school. We didn't want to go, and our parents literally forced us. We played hooky as often as we could. I even remember jumping out of the window to get away from the school.

"Now I wonder whether we were so wise. We wanted to Americanize in a hurry. We were ashamed of the old ways. We didn't want to speak Japanese or know about the history and culture of Japan. But we didn't know what we were looking for. Americanization to us meant big cars, Hollywood-type houses. Now I feel we lost something."

A Chinese candlemaker at work in Honolulu

America's closer ties with Japan have taken the curse off interest in things Japanese or in tours of Japan by local residents. The new concern for increasing American influence in Asia resulted in the sudden discovery that the United States had all too few experts in Oriental languages and culture, and that Hawaii was a major source of personnel for government agencies and business firms active in the Far East. Newspapers, which during the war exhorted Hawaii's Japanese to "talk American," have now carried editorials deploring the disappearance of the Japanese and Chinese languages among the state's young generation. What was once a badge of shame has now become for many a passport to a good job. A prominent Honolulu businessman, with interests throughout Asia, tells an amusing experience which illustrates the point:

"A few days ago I interviewed girls for a new position. All racial groups are welcomed. First to arrive was an attractive second- or third-generation Japanese girl. I asked if she spoke Japanese. She smiled prettily and said, 'Not a word.' The next

A Chinese family in Honolulu celebrates the Festival of the Moon in traditional style

young lady was Caucasian, the daughter of a retired Army officer. Almost automatically I asked, 'Do you speak other languages?' She replied, 'Yes, I speak and write Japanese fluently.' "

Oriental languages are now emphasized at the University of Hawaii. They are offered as optional courses in the public high schools, and they are taught in more concentrated fashion in the various private language schools which were reopened after the war. There are now about one hundred Japanese language schools with some 15,000 students; there are also seven Chinese schools, and one each in Filipino and Korean. There are Japanese and Chinese daily and weekly newspapers, and Korean and Filipino weeklies.

While Chinese and Japanese traditions and customs are not played up as much as the Hawaiian, there has been an increasing tendency both by the press and the Hawaii Visitors Bureau to call attention to the Oriental element in the culture. Festivals and dances of the different nationalities, long ignored, are now be-

A young Japanese girl participates in a summer dance festival

A recent Japanese winner at a multiracial beauty contest at the University of Hawaii

Korean dancer in full ancestral costume

coming more popular. Classes have been started on Maui, with the co-operation of local union officials, to teach Okinawan dances to the descendants of immigrants from that Pacific island. Even among European groups in Hawaii there is a greater interest in their old cultures. The Portuguese, most assimilated of the groups which originally came over as plantation laborers, have been reviving their folk dances and customs.

It is doubtful whether even Japanese and Chinese will survive for very many years as living languages in Hawaii, and there is even a question as to how much of the old culture will remain within a generation or two. The Japanese or Chinese child balks at learning the language of his forefathers only a little less than did his parents. Orientals born in Hawaii consider themselves Americans, and their ties with the mother countries are slender indeed. But there is among the younger generation of Japanese and Chinese more interest in their cultural heritage, and it is as

While national costumes like these are still worn on special occasions, the trend in Hawaii is toward cultural fusion

an influence on the whole life of the islands that the Orient is still potent.

Students of language find especially fascinating the spoken English of the islands, which reflects unmistakably the different national backgrounds of Hawaii's peoples. There are still hangovers from the pidgin developed as a matter of necessity by the immigrant plantation laborers. Pidgin has its own vocabulary, its own structure, its own intonations; and it is not easy for the uninitiated to understand. As a quickly improvised lingual medium of exchange, pidgin served a useful purpose. But it still persists today, long after its original purpose has ceased to exist. It is quite common among school children, sometimes as their own gesture of defiance to school and parental authority. I have met many children whose English reflects quite strongly the influence of pidgin, although their parents speak excellent English. Educators, however, assured me that pidgin is gradually dying out and that in another generation or two it will be a thing of the past.

Quite apart from pidgin is the special flavor of much of the English spoken in Hawaii, and I mean the perfectly correct and grammatical English. The speech of well-educated Orientals often has a subtly different intonation, marked among other things by a rising inflection at the end of sentences. Many Hawaiian words have already found their way into the language, and it is not unlikely that at least some Oriental words will too. The ultimate result may be a regional speech in Hawaii which is perfectly good English but which has its own flavor, as distinctive as the speech of the South or of New England.

Probably the long-term trend is toward cultural fusion and the gradual end of independent, self-generating Oriental and other national cultures in Hawaii. Dr. Lind has suggested that just as the peoples of Hawaii are becoming one through intermarriage so are their cultures fusing and becoming one at an even faster rate. The real issue seems to be whether the Hawaiian and Oriental cultures will simply be swallowed up in a pale Hawaiian copy of mainland influences – or whether they will become part of a new and more colorful culture.

The evidence thus far is encouraging. The old pressure for quick assimilation and Americanization has eased up. Hawaii is part of America, and its emerging culture is American.

12. A Modern Community

Don't look for grass shacks when you come to Hawaii. The primitive way of life is gone forever. The citizens of the new state live a modern life in modern communities with all the modern conveniences and inconveniences.

In fact, and this probably surprises many visitors, the population of Hawaii is primarily urban. Well over half the people in the state live in Honolulu, a city of some 310,000 in 1959 and still growing. Close to another 150,000 live in outlying areas of Oahu, some of them essentially suburbs of Honolulu. About a quarter of the population lives on the neighbor islands. But even here life is not rural. People live in small cities and towns for the most part, and that includes the plantation workers.

The pace of business life is a little slower in Honolulu than in Western cities such as San Francisco, not to speak of New York. People do not seem as much in a hurry on the downtown streets. The climate tends to ease the pressures of a business civilization. Clothes are light and informal. Office hours start earlier than on the mainland, 7:30 or 8 in the morning, and end earlier, 4 or 4:30 in the afternoon. The effect is to cut down the working hours during the hotter part of the day, and also to provide more time for leisure.

Honolulu is essentially a middle-class city, and becoming more

Honolulu seen from the air. At right is Punchbowl, site of the National Cemetery of the Pacific. Center back is the famous Nuuanu Pali pass where Kamehameha I fought the battle that won the island of Oahu for his kingdom

so. It is a service and financial center, and its people are largely in white-collar and service trades. Most people in the city fall into the middle-income bracket. More than a third of its households and families are in the $4,000 to $7,000 a year group. There is a substantial group in the less than $4,000 category, and a group of almost the same size in the over $7,000 group.

Except for agricultural workers on the plantations who receive wages above the average, wages are generally lower than on the mainland — and the cost of living is computed as about twenty percent higher. But some people believe that official statistics underplay factors that make living costs lower in Hawaii; there is no need for indoor heating or for warm winter clothing. On the other hand, housing is expensive.

Most people live in small private homes, not too different from

Fishing enthusiasts find their own secluded nook

those common on our west coast, and the rate of home ownership is very high. In recent years there has been a rapid increase in apartment-house construction. But there remains an acute housing shortage, especially for the middle-income group. Housing developments are being rushed to completion to provide for this group. But housing costs are high because of the shortage of available land.

There are some bad slums in Honolulu and in some communities on the leeward or western side of the island. But several major slum-clearance projects are under way and will provide housing for low-income groups.

The general trend is outward toward the suburbs, toward what were once the outskirts of Honolulu and even farther. Windward or eastern Oahu is now booming with new housing projects and developments. Even the shopping center of Honolulu is moving increasingly out of the downtown area and toward Waikiki in the new Ala Moana shopping area.

Modern freeways intersect Honolulu and provide fast transportation around Oahu. New highways are being built on Hawaii's main island. Traffic and parking are problems in Honolulu as in most cities. But the accident rate is still lower than on the mainland, and automobile insurance is substantially lower. Honolulu has excellent public bus transportation, although this is not true of the neighbor islands.

Generally, Honolulu residents do not frequent Waikiki when they want to go to the beach, although Prince Kuhio Park at Waikiki has an excellent and popular swimming beach. Many of them prefer to find more secluded little hide-outs of their own – like Hanauma Bay only a little distance out of the city, which is formed by the crater of a long dormant volcano. There are many little beaches like this, semicircular with coral reefs, both on Oahu and on other islands.

Oahu as the main population center has a string of forty-nine public beach parks and a network of well-developed recreation facilities. Kapiolani Park, Honolulu's largest, has archery, tennis, and golf areas, as well as the Waikiki Shell, the Waikiki Aquarium, and the Honolulu Zoo. Instead of being admonished by the "Keep off the Grass" signs of many mainland parks, the public is advised, "This Is a Public Park – Have Fun." Park facilities are not so well developed on some of the neighbor islands. State planning officials have been warning that as population and tourism grow more parks will be needed.

Of course, there are many people in Honolulu who rarely go to the beach and do not even seem particularly tanned. But the emphasis by and large is on more outdoor living than is common on the mainland, except perhaps for Southern California. Barbecue cooking in backyards is widespread. Beach picnics, some of them attempting simplified versions of luaus, are frequent.

Swimming, fishing, boating, and water sports are popular with most people, both on Oahu and on the other islands. Duke Kahanamoku, who became the world's swimming champion at the Stockholm Olympic Games in 1912, symbolizes the continuing prowess of the islanders in the water; as sheriff of the city and

Prize-winning Castle & Cooke Terminals Clerks in an ILWU Basketball League

county of Honolulu, he is still a popular figure. Bowling, basketball, baseball, and football are all favorites. Golf enjoys unusual popularity, and is far from a rich man's sport in Hawaii. Many plantation workers play golf and their trade union has an annual golf tournament as well as softball and bowling competitions.

Most people in Hawaii are extremely civic-minded. Community organizations and service clubs of all kinds flourish. There are many clubs representing the various racial groups. But there are also many interracial organizations. The West Honolulu Rotary Club, for example, is a veritable league of nations with representatives of all Hawaii's peoples on its membership list.

A catamaran pulls up toward Waikiki Beach

Hawaii's peoples have a better record of participating in elections and political life than most other states. Better than ninety percent voting by registered voters, as in the 1959 state election, is far from unusual.

Government is streamlined in Hawaii. There are city, county, and state governments. But the state government plays a larger role than elsewhere. There is less duplication of services by local government and considerable saving to the taxpayers. There is more centralization of facilities and authority under the state government.

One school board runs the entire educational system. The state Department of Public Instruction has jurisdiction over the schools on all the islands – with over 136,000 pupils and 5,500 teachers in 2,108 schools. As a result, there is more uniformity in the quality of education and less of the waste characteristic of overlapping local school boards. The school curriculum emphasizes the equality of all Hawaii's peoples, and even in the early grades this idea is fostered through the use of records and songs like "Ballad for Americans."

People take their education seriously in Hawaii. There are

Surf-riding enthusiasts catch a wave off Waikiki Beach

70,000 members of the Parent-Teacher Association in Hawaii — out of a population of less than 600,000. There is an active adult education program attached to the schools, with 13,000 persons in 1959 taking English, citizenship, and other courses.

The University of Hawaii, with about 6,000 students, plays an unusually important part in the life of Hawaii, drawing students from all the islands. The university is strong in the study of Asian languages and cultures. It has done original and creative work in sociology and anthropology, using as source materials the remarkable epic of Hawaii's diversified peoples and their ability to get along together. It sponsors studies in scientific agriculture and soil research, marine biology and geophysics. Apparently the population of Hawaii is not yet large enough to support graduate schools in medicine, dentistry, and law, and students seeking to specialize in these fields must go to the mainland. There are, however, colleges of engineering and of nursing. The university is becoming a center for scholars from Asia, and President Laurence H. Snyder sees as one of its major functions the promotion of understanding between East and West.

Hawaii has an excellent library system, capped by the Library of Hawaii in Honolulu. Among the outstanding librarians on the

Young people in Hawaii still enjoy outrigger canoeing

islands are Miss Mabel K. Jackson of The Library of Hawaii, Dr. Carl Stroven of the University of Hawaii, and Miss Carolyn Crawford, Director of Library Services in the Department of Public Instruction. Although population has been declining in the neighbor islands, their county libraries report increases in the number of books borrowed. And the growth of the number of books in the Library of Hawaii has outpaced the population growth on Oahu. Circulation of books by the Library of Hawaii on Oahu increased from 70,000 in 1913 to well over 1,500,000 in

Young members of a church choir

1958. Book stores report higher per capita sales, especially in children's books.

Hawaii's health and welfare services are more centralized than on the mainland. A welfare client on one island receives the same treatment as on any other. An active state Department of Health has contributed to the progress in combating tuberculosis, which once plagued the islands. Although TB is still a problem, the death rate from this disease is now well below the national average. Venereal diseases, a special problem due to the large number of servicemen, is kept under constant watch, and is combated by the State Office of Health Education. Hansen's disease, as leprosy is now called, has been on the wane, and the number of patients released every year is twice the number of new cases. There are thirty hospitals, with about 4,500 beds, but more are needed.

Daily newspapers – two major ones in Honolulu, and one each on the Big Island and on Maui – as well as radio and television keep people in touch with the mainland. There are several TV stations, but one frequent complaint is that they rebroadcast

Japanese priest beats on a drum to accompany prayer rituals, in a Buddhist temple

mainland programs days or weeks late. A stirring major league ball game or world series generates just as much interest in Hawaii as anywhere else in the United States.

Hawaii has an active religious life, and one which reflects its racial and cultural diversity. Professor Mitsuo Aoki, of Hawaii University's department of religion, sums it up: "Take an afternoon tour of Honolulu, and within a radius of less than six miles, one can visit a Buddhist temple, an Hawaiian heiau, a Confucianist or Taoist temple, a Shinto shrine, a Catholic or Episcopalian cathedral, a Jewish temple, a Congregational chapel, and other Protestant churches of over thirty denominations." The Hawaiian Evangelical Association of Congregational Churches, the direct descendant of the old missionary churches, boasts many Hawaiians among its ministers. But the Catholic and Mormon churches have made heavy inroads. The Catholics alone claim forty percent of the total population.

Buddhism is still predominant among the Japanese, although there are many Japanese Christians too. On one occasion I met a

Chinese court in Honolulu Academy of Arts

preacher, a young Japanese Seventh Day Adventist, who was trying to convert a middle-aged Hawaiian couple. Indeed, I found a good deal of religious searching among the younger Japanese. A Japanese university student says he was first a Buddhist, then a Catholic, then took some university courses in religion. Now, he says, he is still "sort of looking over the field before I commit myself to any church; although I firmly believe in Christian principles."

There is considerable religious activity and ferment in Hawaii — and considerable interaction among the different creeds. There is a Young Men's Buddhist Association obviously patterned after the Young Men's Christian Association. Chinese family funerals are in many cases a combination of Christian and Taoist — or ancestor worship — practices. Some Hawaiian churches have a nativist flavor in both prayer and funeral services. Reverend Abraham K. Akaka, pastor of Kawaiahao Church in Honolulu, the "mother church" established by the missionaries, preached a

Honolulu Academy of Arts

sermon after the victory of statehood in which he identified the Hawaiian spirit of aloha with the Christian idea of God. "Aloha is God," he said. "Aloha is the spirit of God seeking to unite what is separated in the world – the power that unites heart with heart, soul with soul, life with life, culture with culture, race with race, nation with nation."

The interplay of different national influences is also the highlight of Hawaii's active cultural life. The aim of much of this activity is eloquently expressed in the dedication statement of purpose of the Honolulu Academy of Arts:

> "That Hawaiians, Americans, Chinese, Japanese, Koreans, Filipinos, North Europeans, South Europeans, and all other people living here, contacting through the channel of art those deep intuitions common to all, may perceive a foundation on which a new culture, enriched by all the old strains, may be built in these Islands."

The Academy attempts to emphasize Oriental, Western, and Pacific art. In its exhibits as well as in its educational work, it

Children of different background get to know each other at an arts and crafts class

attempts to keep alive all three traditions. A number of excellent Japanese and Chinese artists have developed in Hawaii, but the distance of Hawaii from the world art markets in New York City and Paris makes it difficult to keep them there.

There is an effort in architecture to develop a regional style and apply it to residences as well as to official and business buildings. Office buildings often feature frescoes and murals. The Bishop National Bank has made it a particular point to commission original art work for its new branches. Louvres, metal grill work, and the extensive use of gardens give some of Hawaii's business buildings a character of their own. Many of the better homes are in California ranch style, but with an Oriental influence in their sloping roofs and general atmosphere. The lanai, a covered porch or terrace, is a feature of many homes in Hawaii.

The Honolulu Symphony Orchestra under the direction of George Barati has an international reputation, and has been asked by the State Department to tour the Far East. The Oratorio Society has done major works including Verdi's "Requiem Mass." Honegger's modernistic "King David" with narration and dance was performed in 1958 at the Waikiki Shell under the direction

This mural by Jean Charlot depicting Hawaii's history is a feature of the Waikiki branch of the Bishop National Bank. French-born, Charlot was one of the leaders of the Mexican school of muralists. He has lived and worked in Hawaii since 1949

of Shigeru Hotoke. There are several excellent chamber music groups. A festival of folk music in 1959 featured Earl Robinson's "The Lonesome Train" and Shostakovich's "Song of the Forest" as well as Oriental folk songs and dances. There has, of course, been a problem of accustoming Oriental ears to Western music, and Western ears to Oriental music, but apparently with considerable success.

Millions of words have, of course, been written about Hawaii, starting with Herman Melville and Robert Louis Stevenson, Mark Twain, and Jack London. With the exception of James A. Michener's most recent novel, *Hawaii,* however, there has been little literary work on the interrelationship of Hawaii's diverse peoples. Younger writers sometimes try. Two young University of Hawaii teachers at Hilo created something of a sensation with

"Tsunami," a play dealing with the effect of a tsunami, or tidal wave, on a racially mixed group of people thrown together on a water-soaked plantation on the Big Island.

Japanese movies are a very popular item in Honolulu entertainment, and not only among the local Japanese; Japanese samurai or sword-play epics vie with Hollywood horse operas. There are still Oriental theatre productions and a recent presentation by a Chinese group of "Lady Precious Stream" won considerable attention. The Honolulu Community Theatre has set high professional standards. It has produced a number of successful Broadway musicals such as "South Pacific," "Carousel," and "Music Man." Honolulu audiences have often had the opportunity to see shows such as these before they are performed by road companies in most mainland cities.

Almost every aspect of daily life reflects the diversity of peoples and traditions. The variety of different foods is intriguing, and a visitor is never quite sure what to expect. I have eaten spaghetti at a Chinese home and meat loaf at a Japanese home. Japanese friends like to take you to Chinese restaurants, or perhaps to a place specializing in Hawaiian foods. There is a bewildering choice of restaurants, including one restaurant which offers Chinese food and Japanese entertainment.

This diversity and fusing of cultures shows up in the varieties of clothing and house furnishings, and in the striking good looks of the people. There is no attempt in the newspapers or elsewhere to impose Caucasian standards and stereotypes on a predominantly non-Caucasian population. A Chinese women's club may get the featured spot on the society page, although in general Haole society news still predominates. Beauty contests often feature as many as eight or ten queens, one for each of the different nationalities represented. A milk ad is likely to show a smiling Japanese or Chinese baby. An ad by a local airline boosting vacation travel may feature an obviously interracial family. Banks, insurance companies, and other firms will often include photographs of personnel in their ads, making it clear that the employees are of mixed racial background.

On the whole family ties seems to be strong and stable. As

Chinese women demonstrate the art of cooking some of their traditional dishes

everywhere else in the United States, there is much talk in Hawaii about juvenile delinquency. But the rate of crime among young people is lower than in most big mainland cities. The traditional Oriental family pattern was a big factor in keeping crime down. Young Japanese, Chinese, and Koreans were held too tightly under family discipline to indulge in the excesses common elsewhere. Occasionally middle-aged Orientals grumble that the breakdown of close family ties has meant more delinquency. Emphasis in public facilities for delinquents is on training and education.

The beauty of the physical surroundings of Hawaii adds an exciting and at the same time relaxing quality to life. People seem to absorb modern community living but in a less frantic or tense fashion than on the mainland. There is nothing insular or limited about life in Hawaii – except the very fact of living on an island.

13. Into the Future

The changes in Hawaii since World War II have been so dramatic that some people shudder at the thought of what the next decade or two will bring. Population has almost doubled since 1930. One economist predicts it will double again between 1960 and 1980. In 1939 only 520 air passengers came to Hawaii. By 1959 the number of passengers passing through had increased a thousandfold. In 1946 only 15,000 tourists came to Hawaii. By 1959 there were 200,000. Will Hawaii become just another overcrowded vacation resort by 1980?

Roy Kelley, a prominent Waikiki hotel man, made something of a sensation in 1959 with a speech stating flatly that if Hawaii wanted to keep up with the jet-age influx of tourists, the islands would have to go in for a Miami Beach-type of expansion of hotel facilities. Newspapers featured the speech with the headline:

'MIAMI BEACH' BOOM URGED FOR WAIKIKI

Those are fighting words in Hawaii. Not only the more stiff-necked kamaainas but many other residents as well as relative newcomers squirmed when they read it. The only thing that upsets them even more is the suggestion that Hawaii ought to emulate Nevada and legalize gambling. They cherish the thought that Hawaii is different from the major mainland resorts, and they would like to keep it different.

Kalakaua Avenue – main thoroughfare on Waikiki Beach

But increasingly people in Hawaii have had to grapple with the problem of what the jet age will do to the islands and how much of their old charm and character can survive. The problem is made more serious by the realization that Hawaii's economy needs a steady growth of tourism. No other industry can as quickly bring as many dollars into the new state.

In fact, most businessmen and planners agree that Hawaii's future depends in good part at least on its becoming a major vacation and recreation center for the other forty-nine states. The possibilities for attracting more tourists are almost limitless. More than half of the visitors to Hawaii now come from the West Coast states. Most of the tourists are over forty. Jet travel, faster and possibly cheaper, can make Hawaii accessible to the rest of the country. And its appeal is not necessarily confined to the middle-aged.

The airlines are now in the forefront of a campaign for building even more hotels on Waikiki Beach. Yet hotel men, while they favor further development of the beach area, resist what they

Diamond Head Crater as seen from the distance. Waikiki Beach is at the foot of the crater, extending along the coast

fear may be an excessive expansion which will leave them with vacant rooms part of the year.

But there is the problem of where to put more hotels. There isn't much room left on Waikiki. It is possible, however, to make more land by filling in reefs. Henry J. Kaiser has done some of this, and will do more. There is also a long-standing project for a three-hundred-acre "magic island" on the submerged Ala Moana reef which would substantially expand Waikiki Beach. Tourist promoters hope eventually to get the Army to vacate Fort De Russy's valuable beach land, and there has even been some talk of taking over land now used for public parks.

Another approach is to encourage all-year-round tourism and

Diamond Head Crater as seen from the ocean-front lawn of a Waikiki hotel

eliminate the "feast and famine" aspects of the visitor business. Efforts are made to schedule conventions during off-season months. Aloha Week, a time of festivals, street dancing, and luaus, is celebrated in October, with an eye to getting as many visitors as possible to come in the autumn rather than during the summer and winter seasons. There is obviously room for more visitors if the time for their coming is spread out over the year.

For a long time to come Waikiki will continue to be Hawaii's main tourist center. The beach is still beautiful, the sand white, the weather languorous and warm. There is still the thrill of going out on surfboards and in outrigger canoes and catamarans. It is restful lolling on the beach or around the hotel swimming pools. But some people in the tourist business and in the Hawaii Visitors Bureau have begun to wonder about Waikiki's increasingly "honky-tonk" aspects. They wonder whether it will not become so much like other typical mainland resorts that it will discourage many visitors from coming.

There has been some effort to counteract this possibility. The

Entertainers at Waikiki Beach

HVB and other agencies have been putting more emphasis on preserving old Hawaiian temples, on the colorful aspects of the various national festivals, on the attractions of Honolulu's museums, concerts, and theatres. A vacation at Waikiki can have considerable variety, and can be broken up with sight-seeing both on Oahu and the other islands.

There is really plenty of space for expansion of tourism if it is properly used. There are always the unspoiled, lovely outer islands. In the long run, the attraction of these islands to many visitors is bound to increase. There are scores of uncrowded and enchanting vacation spots there. The argument is advanced that tourists don't go much to these islands because of inadequate hotel facilities. On the other hand, hotel facilities have been lacking because there haven't been enough tourists. Sooner or later the vicious circle will be broken. Possibly state aid will be required in one form or another, at least in terms of better roads

This girl with orchids symbolizes for many the glamour and appeal of Hawaii

and more parks and recreational facilities. More federal expenditures may also be needed to improve roads and facilities in the Hawaii National Park which is situated on two islands, in the Haleakala crater area of Maui, and in the volcano area on Hawaii. Planners point out that Oahu itself lacks beach park facilities, that of its one hundred forty-eight miles of coast line only eighteen are taken by state, city, and county beaches while the rest is owned by private estates, individuals, and the military.

There are already some fears that a tourist build-up of the outer islands will make them into replicas of Waikiki. A recent government survey indicates that residents of the beautiful Kona coast of the Big Island want to maintain "the Kona way of life," which they describe as slow, quiet, relaxed, natural, casual, unhurried. The danger to "the Kona way of life" and the beauties and graces of the other islands still seems pretty remote at this point. If there is planning and foresight, Hawaii can accommodate a good many more visitors without losing its basic appeal.

There is another aspect of continuing change in Hawaii which

On the west side of Oahu, away from Waikiki, there is fine camping and fishing at Maile Beach

troubles some people. There has been an influx not only of tourists but also of businessmen and executives from the mainland. In fact, the Caucasian percentage of the population, augmented by newcomers from the mainland, is rapidly increasing. Will this change the aloha spirit? Will it present dangers to the nondiscriminatory pattern of racial relations? Will it result in efforts to whittle down the political and economic role of Hawaii's nonwhite population? To offer definitive answers would be foolhardy. But while fears along these lines may be real enough, there are also factors which operate in favor of preserving the democratic essence of Hawaii's way of life.

One of these is simply that Hawaii's aloha spirit exercises a strong influence on those who come into contact with it. Another is that Hawaii is increasingly becoming a bridge between Asia and America, a commercial, technical, scientific, and cultural link between the two continents. This is expected to work as a counterbalance against the leveling influence of commercialism in

Outrigger canoe on the Kona coast of the Big Island

Hawaii's cultural life, emphasizing instead many of the new state's distinctive and more attractive features. It is also expected to strengthen Hawaii's unique pattern of race relations. For this pattern is the source of Hawaii's appeal to Asia. To undermine it would be to lose a significant American asset.

Hawaii's fleet of islands lies about 2,400 miles from the North American continent, about 4,000 miles from Japan. This is something more than an obvious geographic fact. Hawaii is becoming a great world crossroads between Asia and America.

Here stop the passengers on countless ships and planes between the two continents. Visitors to the United States from Japan and other Asian countries often stop over in Hawaii, and many find the new state a place worth visiting in its own right. American business firms interested in the possibilities of a growing Asian

There are big ones off the Kona coast

market for their products are establishing branches in Honolulu. Engineering, technical, and construction firms are considering using Honolulu as a base for operations in Asia; some are already doing so.

Hawaii, with a population about three quarters nonwhite and more than half Asian, is also a crossroads between American and Asian cultures and peoples. President Laurence H. Snyder of the University of Hawaii has suggested an $84,000,000 International University, aimed at creating a meeting ground between Asian and American scholars. The proposal has received influential backing from Senate Majority Leader Lyndon B. Johnson as well as from Governor Quinn.

For several years there has been active in Hawaii the International Co-operation Center financed largely by the federal government's International Co-operation Administration. Since 1954 it has serviced several thousand representatives of thirty countries, providing education and training for many as well as hospitality and assistance. Some have come to Hawaii, to the center, sponsored by the World Health Organization or by a foreign government. Others have come as individuals or under the sponsorship of private agencies and business firms. To it have come nurses from Costa Rica, educators from Nepal, telecommunications engineers from Vietnam, home economists from Japan, entomologists from Greece and Nicaragua, bankers from Korea and Cambodia. Programs at the center have provided a form of technical aid for underdeveloped countries.

In Hawaii is to be found at least part of the answer to the official ignorance about Asia disclosed in the best-selling novel *The Ugly American*, to the lack of concern among some United States diplomats for the culture and traditions of the nations of the Far East. Here are Americans who are Asian in background, men and women who understand Asia and know its languages. Americans of Oriental ancestry in Hawaii have been increasingly employed by the State Department and the International Co-operation Administration for missions abroad.

Take the case of Professor James S. Miyake of the University of Hawaii, grandson of plantation laborers who came over as immigrants from Japan, son of a mechanic. Several years ago he went to Burma to a conference of UNESCO – the United Nations Educational, Scientific and Cultural Organization. He arrived just as the first session was getting under way, and everyone was looking for the American representatives. The chairman looked right past Professor Miyake. His presence was helpful to United States prestige at the conference and he was able to get a more intimate view of life in Burma than would have been possible for a Caucasian. In 1959 Miyake went to Thailand as director of the United States Educational Foundation, sponsored by the Thai and United States governments in co-operation with the Fulbright Foundation. Men like Professor Miyake help prove to Asia that

American democracy can be real and vital for people whose skins don't happen to be white.

Much of Hawaii's future rests on its position in the Pacific between Asia and America and on its unique interracial population. It has already helped to promote understanding between East and West, and political leaders both in Honolulu and Washington believe that it will continue to do so, playing a major role for peace in the Pacific by helping to promote trade, scientific and cultural relations.

Hawaii's example may not only help convince Asians that American democracy works. It may also convince many Americans of the same thing. Certainly Hawaii should serve to show Americans of good will throughout the country, including the South, that racial supremacy is a thing of the past. In Hawaii they will find the proof that Americans of different racial backgrounds can live and work together in harmony and in equality.

Hawaii has been called our "diplomatic state." It has been called our "showcase of democracy." It has most frequently been called our "Paradise of the Pacific." It is all of these, and in this combination lies its unique appeal to the peoples who make their home there, to tourists from the mainland, and to its visitors from many lands.

Tips for Travelers

Tips for Travelers

VISITING HAWAII

Hawaii can be reached from anywhere in the United States by plane, and from the West Coast by steamship. Plane travel offers the advantages of speed and economy, while an ocean cruise provides greater rest and luxury.

Airlines with regular flights to Honolulu are Canadian Pacific Airlines, Japan Airlines, Northwest Orient Airlines, Pan American World Airways, Qantas Empire Airways, Transocean Air Lines, and United Air Lines. Tourist excursion round-trip fare on the major air lines starts at $232 from San Francisco, somewhat less by Transocean, a supplemental line, and runs to $338 on a first-class flight. From New York the lowest round-trip rate on regular air lines is $400. Flight time from the West Coast is from eight to ten hours. Faster jet service began in September 1959.

Major steamship lines serving Hawaii from the West Coast are American President Lines and Matson Lines. There are also sailings via the Hawaiian Steamship Company and Orient Lines. Lowest Matson rates start at $145 one way, while American President Lines offers some dormitory-style tourist accommodations starting at about $100. Most accommodations range considerably higher. Voyages last about four and one-half days.

All-expense tours from San Francisco, including air transportation, start at about $350 per person for eight days. There is some saving on tours if families or groups of friends go together. The variety of tours offered in Hawaii is almost infinite, depending on time, taste, and money. Many people take care of their own transportation to Hawaii, and then arrange for tours of Oahu and of the neighbor islands from Honolulu. Any travel agency will make tour arrangements.

Another possibility is for families or groups to see Hawaii on their own, with only occasional help from tourist guides. This is most practical if one has friends or business associates in Hawaii – although the Hawaii Visitors Bureau is always available for advice and information.

Once you get to Hawaii, travel is no problem. Interisland service, by Hawaiian Airlines and Aloha Airlines, is fast and surprisingly inexpensive. Facilities for renting automobiles are available everywhere. It is also possible to get cabs and limousines both for short and long trips.

Hotel accommodations in Hawaii vary considerably in price and luxury. It is possible to get modest but adequate hotel rooms for as little as $5 a night per person – or for $30 and up. Prices are not out of line, and compare rather favorably on the whole with comparable mainland hotels.

Perhaps two bits of advice are in order to first-time visitors to Hawaii:

1. See as much as you can both of Oahu and the neighbor islands. You will not really see Hawaii if you stay exclusively at Waikiki Beach. If your finances are limited, it is possible to stay at lower-price hotels and spend the money thus saved by visiting the neighbor islands.

2. You can get all the information you want on hotels, tours, hunting, fishing, or anything else about Hawaii from the Hawaii Visitors Bureau, 2051 Kalakaua Avenue, Honolulu, Hawaii. You can probably make your trip more enjoyable by consulting HVB.

SIGHTSEER'S GUIDE

The Hawaii Visitors Bureau has compiled this list of places of interest on each of the major islands, along with a guide to pronunciation of Hawaiian place names. The pronunciation guide follows the specific place of interest and is in parentheses.

OAHU ISLAND

OAHU ISLAND (OH-AH-HOO) *Capital island of major Hawaiian chain, also called the Aloha Isle.*

HONOLULU (HOH-NOH-LOO-LOO) *Capital city, site of Waikiki Beach and Honolulu International Airport.*

ACADEMY OF ARTS *Art exhibits, site of orchid shows.*

ALA MOANA (AH-LAH MOH-AH-NA) *Honolulu seaside park, site of reconstructed Hawaiian village of grass huts. Favorite picnic spot.*

ALA WAI (AH-LAH-WAI) *Canal "back door" of Waikiki that leads to yacht harbor.*

ALOHA TOWER (A-LOH-HAH) *Famous Honolulu harbor landmark, observation platform.*

ARCHIVES OF HAWAII *Most complete Hawaiiana collection in the United States.*

BISHOP MUSEUM *Largest collection of Pacificana in world.*

THE BLOW HOLE *Hole in lava ledge through which ocean "geysers."*

DIAMOND HEAD CRATER *Extinct volcano, famous Waikiki landmark.*

HANAUMA BAY (HAH-NAW-MAH) *Scenic swimming spot in remains of old crater.*

HONGWANJI TEMPLE (HONG-WAHN-JEE) *Buddhist temple in mid-Honolulu.*

HONOLULU HALE (HOH-NO-LOO-LOO HAH-LEE) *City Hall, site of pageantry and exhibits.*

IOLANI BARRACKS (EE-OH-LAH-NEE) *Housed Royal Household Guards during monarchy.*

IOLANI PALACE (EE-OH-LAH-NEE) *Only royal palace in the United States.*

JUDICIARY BUILDING *Former parliament building of kingdom.*

KAILUA (KAI-LOO-AH) *Windward residential area near beach.*

FOSTER PARK BOTANICAL GARDENS *Rare tropical trees and plants, fine orchid collection, open daily gratis.*

KALAKAUA AVENUE (KAH-LAH-KOW-AH) *Waikiki's main avenue and shopping center.*

KANEOHE BAY (KAH-NEH-OH-EH) *Windward fishing and sailing grounds near yacht club.*

KAWAIAHAO CHURCH (KAH-WAI-HAH-OH) *Westminster Abbey of the kingdom.*

KING KAMEHAMEHA'S STATUE (KA-MEH-HAH-MEH-HAH) *Favorite subject for photographers.*

KOKO HEAD CRATER (KOH-KOH) *Prominent landmark at eastern tip of Oahu.*

KOOLAU MOUNTAINS (KOH-OH-LAU) *Volcanic chain, backdrop for Honolulu.*

KUKANILOKE (KOO-KAH-NEE-LOH-KOH) *Sacred birthstones in pineapple field.*

LAIE TEMPLE (LAH-EE-EH) *Mormon temple in tropical setting.*

MISSION HOUSES *Museums and oldest frame house in Hawaii.*

NATIONAL MEMORIAL CEMETERY OF THE PACIFIC *Burial grounds for dead of World War II and Korea in extinct crater. Scene of Easter sunrise services.*

NUUANU AVENUE (NOO-OO-AH-NOO) *Leads through battleground of ancient kings.*

NUUANU PALI (NOO-OO-AH-NOO PAH-LEE) *2,000-foot gap in Koolau range, Oahu's most famous scenic view.*

PEARL HARBOR *Home of United States Pacific Fleet.*

PUU-O-MAHUKA (POO-OO-OH-MAH-HOO-KAH) *Ruins of largest Hawaiian temple on Oahu.*

PETROGLYPH PARK *Ancient Hawaiian stone drawings behind Royal Mausoleum.*

QUEEN EMMA'S HOME *Museum with queen's memorabilia.*

QUEEN KAPIOLANI PARK (KAH-PEE-OH-LAH-NEE) *Site of outdoor bandshell, tennis courts, zoo, polo grounds, and hula festival.*

ROYAL MAUSOLEUM *Burying ground for Hawaiian kings.*

SACRED FALLS (KAH-LEE-OO-WAH-AH) *87-foot waterfall in Kaliuwaa Valley.*

UNIVERSITY OF HAWAII *Excels in tropical agriculture, marine biology, Pacific and Asian cultures. Beautiful tropical campus.*

WAIANAE MOUNTAINS (WAI-AH-NA-EH) *Range parallels Oahu's southwest coast.*

WAIKIKI (WAI-KEE-KEE) *Suburb of Honolulu, bounded by ocean, a canal, and a volcano. 4,000 permanent residents.*

WAIKIKI AQUARIUM (WAI-KEE-KEE) *World's most beautiful, displays tropical marine life.*

WAIKIKI BEACH (WAI-KEE-KEE) *Year-round resort center with hotels and shops and apartment buildings; 226 acres of public beaches.*

WASHINGTON PLACE *Colonial residence of governor, near palace.*

HAWAII ISLAND

HAWAII ISLAND (HAH-WAI-EE) *Also called The Big Island, The Volcano Island, The Orchid Island. 4,030 square miles, 65 minutes by plane from Honolulu. One of largest centers of orchid culture in world.*

HILO (HEE-LO) *Principal city and main port of Hawaii Island.*

AKAKA FALLS (AH-KAH-KAH) *420-foot waterfall in park, favorite picnic site.*

HAWAII NATIONAL PARK (HAH-WAI-EE) *Scenic fern forests, desert lands, lava tubes, etc.*

HONAUNAU (HOH-NAU-NAU) *Remains of walled City of Refuge and sacred temple, soon to be part of Hawaii National Park.*

HONOKAA (HOH-NOH-KAH-AH) *Big Island's second city near steep valley of Waipio.*

HULIHEE PALACE (HOO-LEE-HEH) *Now museum of Hawaiiana with Hawaiian guide.*

KEALAKEKUA BAY (KEH-AH-LAH-KEH-KOO-AH) *Spot where Captain Cook lost his life.*

KILAUEA (KI-LAH-EH-A) *Active crater in Hawaii National Park.*

LAUPAHOEHOE (LAH-PAH-HOY-HOY) *Early boat landing along sugar coast, built on old lava flow.*

LILIUOKALANI PARK (LEE-LEE-OO-OH-KA-LAH-NEE) *Beautiful Japanese garden near bay.*

KONA DISTRICT (KOH-NA) *Home of coffee industry, deep-sea fishing center.*

MAUNA KEA (MAW-NAH-KEH-A) *Dormant volcano in Hawaii National Park.*

MAUNA LOA (MAW-NAH-LO-A) *Active volcano in Hawaii National Park.*

NAHA STONE (NAH-HA) *Testing rock for would-be kings.*

ORCHID SPRINGS *Warm crystal swimming pool, volcanically heated.*

PUNA DISTRICT (POO-NAH) *Black sand beach, green lake, scene of recent volcanic eruption.*

WAIMEA PLATEAU (WAI-MEH-A) *Home of Hawaii's cattle industry and second largest ranch in United States.*

MAUI ISLAND

MAUI ISLAND (MAW-EE) *Also called The Valley Isle, second largest of Hawaiian chain, 728 square miles. 40 minutes by plane from Honolulu.*

WAILUKU (WAI-LOO-KOO) *Maui's main city and county seat.*

HALEAKALA (HAH-LEH-AH-KAH-LA) *Scenic mammoth crater 41 miles from Wailuku.*

HANA (HAH-NA) *Secluded tropical Hawaiian village centering around luxurious Hotel Hana-Maui and 10,000-acre Hana Ranch. Has own airport.*

IAO NEEDLE (EE-OW) *2,000-foot rock pinnacle in valley of forest-clad cliffs, favorite of photographers.*

KAHULUI (KAH-HOO-LOO-EE) *Maui's principal seaport. Sugar and pineapple loading.*

KULA UPLANDS (KOO-LA) *Rich farming and grazing lands on slopes of Haleakala, English-style manor house puts up visitors.*

LAHAINA (LAH-HAI-NA) *Sugar and pineapple plantation town and resort, former harbor for whalers. Site of Lahainaluna* (LAH-HAI-NA-LOO-NA), *oldest school west of Rockies.*

KAUAI ISLAND

KAUAI ISLAND (KOW-AI) *Also called The Garden Island. Fourth largest of Hawaiian chain, 555 square miles. 40 minutes by air from Honolulu.*

LIHUE (LEE-HOO-EH) *Largest center of population and county seat.*

BARKING SANDS *Coral and lava beach sands that "bark" when rubbed together.*

HAENA (HAH-EH-NA) *Site of legendary dry cave near beautiful beach of same name.*

HOLO-HOLO-KU (HOH-LOH-HOH-LOH-KOO) *Remains of ancient Hawaiian temple near royal birthstones.*

KALALAU (KAH-LAH-LAU) *Spectacular green valley immortalized by Jack London story.*

KIKIAOLA (KEE-KEE-AH-OH-LAH) *Ancient Hawaiian watercourse of fitted lava stones.*

KOKEE (KOH-KEH) *Summer resort area on cool mountain plateau with forest reserves.*

KOLOA (KOH-LOH-A) *Site of first Hawaii sugar plantation.*

MENEHUNE (MEN-EH-HOO-NEH) *Legendary dwarfs who built mammoth, hand-fitted stone works overnight.*

MENEHUNE FISH POND (MEN-EH-HOO-NEH) *Great lava stone pond attributed to menehune skill, favorite of photographers.*

NAWILIWILI (NAH-WEE-LEE-WEE-LEE) *Picturesque port near Lihue.*

PA'U-A-LAKA (PAH-OO-AH-LAH-KA) *One of world's most unusual gardens open to public. Rare cacti, orchids and plumeria.*

POIPU BEACH (POY-POO) *Fine swimming and surfing beach near Spouting Horn sea "geyser."*

WAIALEALE (WAI-AH-LEH-AH-LEH) *Highest mountain on Kauai.*

WAILUA RIVER (WAI-LOO-A) *Navigable by small boats for four miles inland, where visitors explore fern-curtained lava grotto.*

WAIMEA (WAI-MEH-A) *Historic town at mouth of Waimea Canyon on Waimea River.*

WAIMEA CANYON (WAI-MEH-A) *Kauai's most spectacular view, miniature "Grand Canyon."*

MOLOKAI ISLAND

MOLOKAI ISLAND (MOH-LOH-KAI) *Also called The Friendly Isle. Fifth in size of Hawaiian group, 260 square miles. 35 minutes by air from Honolulu.*

HALAWA VALLEY (HAH-LAH-VAH) *Favorite of the off-trail camera explorer.*

KALAUPAPA PENINSULA (KAH-LAU-PAH-PA) *Home of Kalaupapa settlement for Hansen's Disease. Population about 280 persons, including medical and religious workers.*

KAMAKAU (KAH-MAH-KAU) *4,970-foot volcano, highest on Molokai.*

KAUNAKAKAI (KAU-NAH-KAH-KAI) *Small harbor for pineapple and cattle-loading.*

PENGUIN BANK *Submarine shelf portion of Molokai, 27 miles long, rich fishing grounds.*

LANAI ISLAND

LANAI ISLAND (LAH-NAI) *Also called The Pineapple Island. Sixth in size of Hawaiian chain, 141 square miles. Planted almost exclusively to pineapples.*

LANAI CITY (LAH-NAI) *Chief city located on 1,400-foot plateau below Lanaihale Mountain.*

KAUMALAPAU (KAU-MAH-LAH-PAU) *Principal port for pineapple loading.*

PALAWAI (PAH-LAH-WAI) *Ancient crater 3½ miles in diameter.*

NIIHAU ISLAND

NIIHAU ISLAND (NEE-HAU) *Privately owned Hawaiian Island not open to visitors, seventh in size of Hawaiian chain. Largest colony of pure-blooded Hawaiians.*

FESTIVALS OF HAWAII

Hawaii's festivals and holidays reflect its varied national and cultural influences. Here is a list compiled by the Hawaii Visitors Bureau.

JANUARY: 1 – New Year's Day in Hawaii is celebrated as elsewhere, but has some special features such as fireworks displays.
Last Saturday of every month (except December) is the usual date for Hukilaus, old-time fishing festivals.
17 – Start of Narcissus Festival.

FEBRUARY: Narcissus Festival, January 17 through February 13. This is the Chinese New Year celebration, based on the Chinese lunar calendar. The name comes from the white "spirit lilies" which symbolize good fortune, and is a time of lion dances, Mandarin banquets, Oriental pageantry, fireworks.
Ka Palapala Beauty Pageant, usually at end of February, is the University of Hawaii's annual beauty contest in which seven beauty queens are named for seven nationalities.

MARCH: 3 – Japanese Girls' Day or Doll Festival – Display of dolls and Japanese culture to honor the birth and happiness of daughters. From the custom of sending dolls and gifts to baby girl on first March 3 after her birth. Dolls are put away on her thirteenth birthday and not brought out until her marriage.
15 – Start of the Cherry Blossom Festival.
26 – Kuhio Day, territorial holiday to honor the birthday anniversary of Prince Kuhio, second delegate to Congress from Hawaii.
Easter Sunrise Service at Punchbowl National Cemetery of the Pacific.

APRIL: Cherry Blossom Festival, March 15 to mid-April. Japanese Spring Festival celebrated with culture shows, pageants, sports, drama, stage show from Japan.

First Sunday – Wesak Day Flower Festival commemorates Buddha's birthday anniversary. Held at Kapiolani Park.
Festival of Folk Music, early April. Theme of festival is "East Meets West in Hawaii." Concerts at Waikiki Shell.

MAY: 1 – Lei Day, only fete of its kind in the world, dedicated to the lei as symbol of Hawaiian friendship, aloha, natural beauty. At Waikiki Shell.
5 – Boys' Day, when Japanese families honor their male offspring with flying colorful paper carp.
Hawaiian Song Festival, on a Sunday in May, presenting original Hawaiian songs for prizes held in public park.
Hibiscus Show, a one-day May event at Ala Moana Park.
Big Game Fishing Derby – Last week-end of May, off Oahu.

JUNE: 1 – Rainbow Trout Season opens on Kauai Island.
11 – Kamehameha Day, commemorating the life of King Kamehameha, first ruler of all islands.

JULY: 50th State Fair, in late June and early July, at Waikiki Shell, Kapiolani Park.
4th of July – Celebrated in islands as elsewhere in the United States, with evening symphony concert and fireworks at Waikiki Shell.
Every week-end through July and August – Bon Dances, mass Buddhist dances to honor the dead, locations announced each week.
25 – Children's Folk Dance Festival at Waikiki Shell.
Canoe Regattas at Waikiki and Kailua, Oahu, in late July.

AUGUST: Sunday Hula Festivals at Waikiki Shell.
Every week-end – Bon Dances continue.

SEPTEMBER: Chinese Moon Festival. The date usually falls in September. Commemorates the visit of Emperor Ming Huan to Paradise with moon-cake displays and pageants.

OCTOBER: Mid-October through mid-November – Aloha Week, the largest of all Hawaiian Festivals, the "Mardi Gras of the Pacific" with pageantry, street-dancing, hula festivals, luaus, balls, parades.

NOVEMBER: Thanksgiving Day, with annual football game at Honolulu Stadium, Thanksgiving luaus.
Last of November to December – International Surfing Championships at Makaha, Oahu island.

DECEMBER: Sunday closest to December 7 – Bodhi Day, anniversary of the enlightenment of Buddha and the establishment of Buddhism. Buddhist rituals.

19 – Princess Bernice Pauahi Bishop's birthday anniversary, observed with ceremonies at Royal Mausoleum by Hawaiian societies and Kamehameha Schools.
25 – Christmas, with Santa arriving on surfboard.
31 – New Year's Eve with fireworks.

FISHING AND HUNTING IN HAWAII

Hawaii's fishing and hunting are deservedly popular with visitors. The Hawaii Visitors Bureau has compiled detailed mimeographed reports on the state's fish and fishing facilities and on hunting in Hawaii. These are available free of charge on request.

WHAT TO READ

There is an extensive literature about Hawaii. A list of books and publications has been prepared by the Library of Hawaii for the Hawaii Visitors Bureau. It includes books of general interest as well as some which will appeal to readers with special interests. This list can be obtained on request from the Library of Hawaii and the Hawaii Visitors Bureau.